TABLE SAW
TECHNIQUES

Use Your Saw Like a Pro

by Chris Marshall

CREATIVE
PUBLISHING
international

CHANHASSEN, MINNESOTA

www.creativepub.com

CONTENTS

© Copyright 2003
Creative Publishing international, Inc.
18705 Lake Drive East
Chanhassen, Minnesota 55317
1-800-328-3895
www.creativepub.com
All rights reserved

Printed by Quebecor World
10 9 8 7 6 5 4 3 2 1

President/CEO: Michael Eleftheriou
Vice President/Publisher: Linda Ball
Vice President/Retail Sales & Marketing: Kevin Haas

Executive Editor: Bryan Trandem
Creative Director: Tim Himsel
Managing Editor: Michelle Skudlarek
Editorial Director: Jerri Farris

Author: Chris Marshall
Editors: Brett Martin, Karen Ruth
Copy Editor: Karen Ruth
Technical Photo Editor: Randy Austin
Mac Production: Jon Simpson
Illustrators: Jon Simpson, Earl Slack
Photo Researcher: Julie Caruso
Studio Services Manager: Jeanette Moss McCurdy
Photographer: Tate Carlson
Scene Shop Carpenters: Jacob Austin, Randy Austin
Director of Production Services and Photography: Kim Gerber
Production Manager: Helga Thielen

TABLE SAW TECHNIQUES

Other titles from Creative Publishing international include:

The New Everyday Home Repairs; Basic Wiring & Electrical Repairs; Building Decks; Home Masonry Projects & Repairs; Workshop Tips & Techniques; Bathroom Remodeling; Flooring Projects & Techniques; Decorative Accessories; Kitchen Accessories; Maximizing Minimal Space; Outdoor Wood Furnishings; Easy Wood Furniture Projects; Customizing Your Home; Carpentry: Remodeling; Carpentry: Tools • Shelves • Walls • Doors; Exterior Home Repairs & Improvements; Home Plumbing Projects & Repairs; Advanced Home Wiring; Advanced Deck Building; Built-In Projects for the Home; Landscape Design & Construction; Refinishing & Finishing Wood; Building Porches & Patios; Advanced Home Plumbing; Remodeling Kitchens; Finishing Basements & Attics; Stonework & Masonry Projects; Sheds, Gazebos & Outbuildings; Building & Finishing Walls & Ceilings; Customizing Your Home; The Complete Guide to Home Plumbing; The Complete Guide to Home Wiring; The Complete Guide to Building Decks; The Complete Guide to Painting & Decorating; The Complete Guide to Creative Landscapes; The Complete Guide to Home Masonry; The Complete Guide to Home Carpentry; The Complete Guide to Home Storage; The Complete Guide to Windows & Doors; The Complete Guide to Bathrooms; The Complete Guide to Easy Woodworking Projects; The Complete Guide to Flooring; The Complete Guide to Ceramic & Stone Tile; The Complete Photo Guide to Home Repair; The Complete Photo Guide to Home Improvement; The Complete Photo Guide to Outdoor Home Improvement; Accessible Home; Open House; Lighting Design & Installation

Library of Congress
 Cataloging-in-Publication Data on file
ISBN 1-58923-097-3

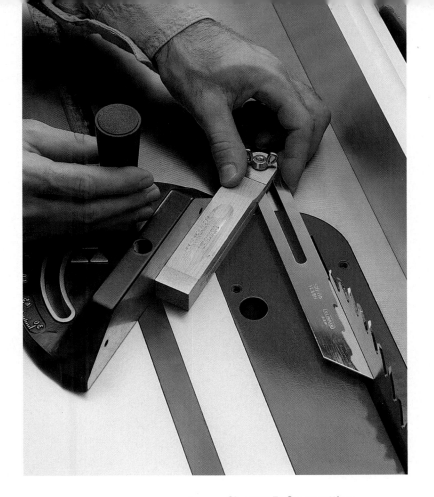

INTRODUCTION

Whether you are an occasional workshop putterer, an aspiring woodworker, or a homeowner with a penchant for doing things yourself, a table saw belongs in your workshop. No other saw cuts as efficiently or accurately, and few woodworking machines are as versatile. If you haven't purchased a table saw yet, here are several real shop scenarios that are probably familiar frustrations: Are you still "eyeballing" your rip and crosscuts by guiding a circular saw along a layout line? If so, you know that accuracy is only as good as your aim and a steady hand behind the tool. Ever tried to cut tight miter joints with a handheld saw? Forget it. The angles never form a square corner. How about cutting multiple workpieces the exact same size? A tough proposition, isn't it? Repetitive cutting is nearly impossible to do accurately by hand. Table saws make these essential types of cuts effortlessly and with almost surgical precision.

Table Saw Techniques opens with a chapter on how to choose which saw is right for your needs, how to evaluate a used saw, and what blade choices are best for your purposes. The second chapter covers setting up your workshop in a safe and efficient manner. The next chapter, on tuning your saw, gives you all the information you need to keep your saw running its best. Remaining chapters give detailed directions for particular cutting jobs: ripping, crosscutting, creating joinery, and milling coves and trim.

Every tool needs a thorough reference manual to unleash its potential, and this book was written for that purpose. Hundreds of full-color photographs and carefully written text will guide you every step of the way, making your sawing safer and more enjoyable. Whatever your skill level or project interests may be, keep this handy resource near your saw so you can refer to it again and again. Happy sawing!

NOTICE TO READERS

This book provides useful instructions, but we cannot anticipate all of your working conditions or the characteristics of your materials and tools. For safety, you should use caution, care, and good judgment when following the procedures described in this book. Consider your own skill level and the instructions and safety precautions associated with the various tools and materials shown. The publisher cannot assume responsibility for any damage to property, injury to persons, or losses incurred as a result of misuse of the information provided.

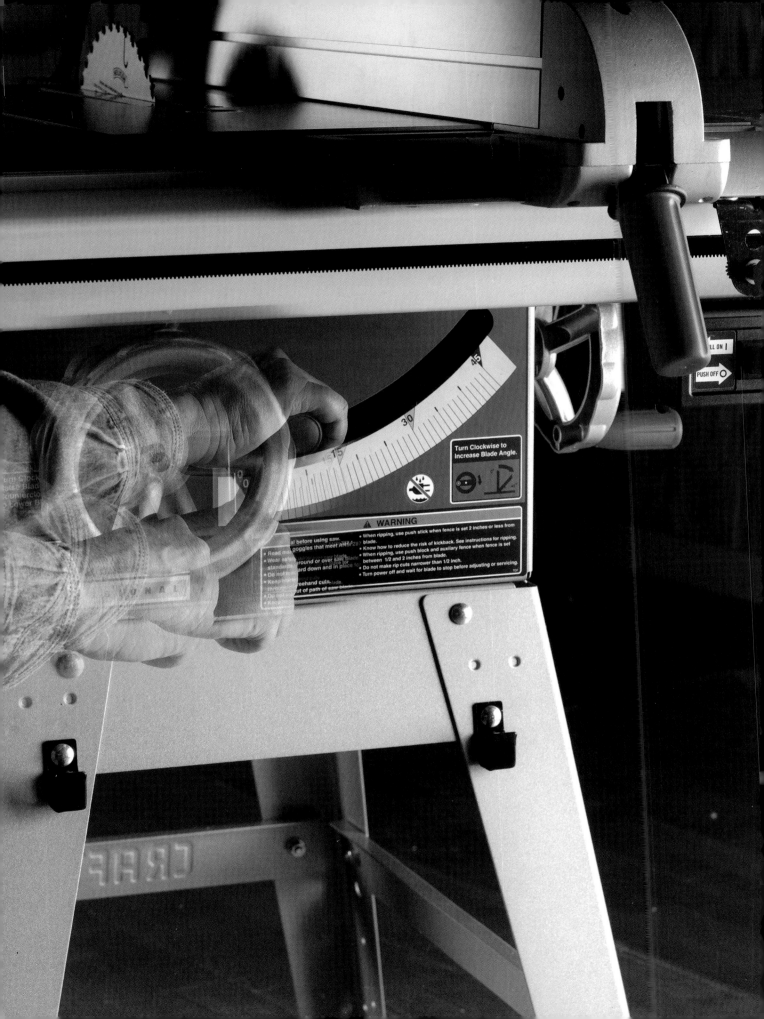

Chapter 1
TABLE SAW OVERVIEW

Next to routers, table saws are the most versatile machines for working wood. As you'll see in the following chapters, table saws are first and foremost cutting tools, but they also earn their keep milling a wide range of woodworking joints, shaping molding or trimwork, and even sanding on occasion. Despite this range of capabilities, a table saw is actually a wonderfully simple machine. Strip away the details that differentiate one type of table saw from the next, and you're left with a flat table, a blade that rises up through it, and a couple of fences running perpendicular and parallel to the blade. Whether you spend $100 or many times that amount on your table saw, the relationship of table, blade, and fences is the same.

You don't have to spend an arm and a leg to buy a table saw, but the old adage of getting what you pay for certainly applies here. Generally speaking, more money buys you higher-quality components, fewer maintenance hassles, and added bells and whistles that can make your sawing more efficient and precise. As prices increase, so do the levels of performance you can expect from the tool. But there's really no substitute for experience—the most expensive saw won't ensure your success or proficiency as a woodworker. Only time and practice can do that for you.

If you haven't purchased a saw yet, this chapter will help steer you through your options. Use these pages to familiarize yourself with the parts of the table saw and the different categories of saws available. You'll also find a section that will help you shop for a used table saw if you don't plan to buy one fresh from the manufacturer. A used table saw can offer great value if you know what pitfalls to avoid.

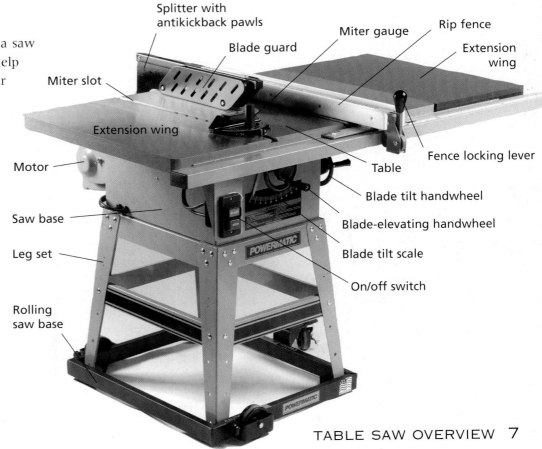

Splitter with antikickback pawls
Miter gauge
Rip fence
Blade guard
Extension wing
Miter slot
Extension wing
Fence locking lever
Motor
Table
Blade tilt handwheel
Saw base
Blade-elevating handwheel
Leg set
Blade tilt scale
On/off switch
Rolling saw base

Rounding out this overview of table saws, we'll cover the essential issues of choosing a saw blade. Even a top-quality table saw won't perform at its peak with an inferior blade. On the other hand, budget-priced saws can exceed their limits, to some degree, by simply installing a sharp carbide-tipped blade with the right tooth geometry. This section will help you select the best blade for both task and tool.

The extension wings on cabinet saws like this one are made of cast iron, which adds weight but helps ensure flatness.

Parts of a table saw

Starting from the top and working downward, here are the primary components of most table saws:

Table & extension wings. Saw tables range in size from little more than 2 feet in length and width to almost twice that size. Tables are wider than they are deep in order to support long workpieces during crosscutting operations. For safety's sake as well as to increase cutting precision and ease of operation, nothing beats a big table. Typically, saw tables consist of three parts: a center section bolted to the saw base, and two extension wings attached to the left and right

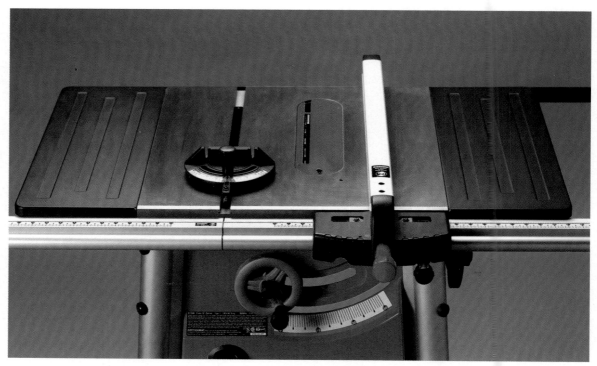

Contractor's saws may have pressed steel extension wings, like the one shown here, or the wings may be webbed or solid cast-iron. Pressed steel wings make suitable bearing surfaces, provided they are adjusted for flatness initially and checked periodically after that.

of center. The center section on floor-standing saws is made of cast iron, while the extension wings may be formed from either cast iron or pressed sheet steel. Cast iron adds more weight to the saw, making the tool heavier to transport and move around the shop. But dense, heavy iron is the best material for dampening vibrations produced by the saw's motor and drivetrain. It also provides a more suitable medium than steel for grinding the table surfaces perfectly flat.

Portable benchtop saws have the smallest saw tables. It's common for these small saws to have one-piece tabletops made of cast aluminum alloy instead of iron. Aluminum sheds pounds, but it's not as scratch-resistant or as hard as iron. It's also less likely to be perfectly flat, although this depends on the casting and how the top is attached to the base.

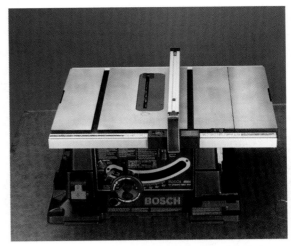

Benchtop saws generally have extension wings made of the same material as the saw table. On this saw, the wings and table are cast aluminum.

Throat plate. Surrounding the blade is a removable throat plate that sits in a shallow recess in the tabletop. The throat plate provides the pass-though slot for the blade. It also serves as a quick way to gain access to the blade arbor nut from above the table when changing blades and performing other maintenance tasks. Better throat plates are outfitted with several Allen screws so the plate can be adjusted flush with the tabletop. One issue with factory throat plates is that the blade slot is made wide enough to accommodate both square and tilted blade angles. This makes the plate versatile, but it also allows the blade to chip and tear out wood fibers in the blade opening area. A solution to this problem is to make your own throat plates instead of using the one that comes with the saw (see page 59).

Miter slots & miter gauge. Most saw tables are outfitted with a pair of grooves, called miter slots, on either side of the blade. Miter slots are parallel

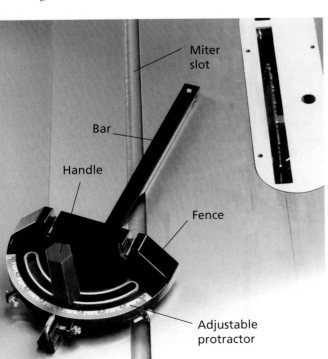

Miter slot

Bar

Handle

Fence

Adjustable protractor

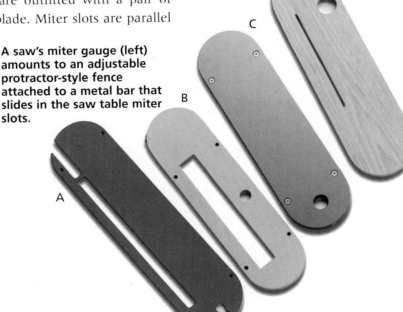

A saw's miter gauge (left) amounts to an adjustable protractor-style fence attached to a metal bar that slides in the saw table miter slots.

Standard-issue throat plates (A) are made of metal, but you can buy them in phenolic or plastic for use with dado blades (B) or as blanks (C) for cutting your own blade slot. It's also easy to make throat plates from wood (D).

to one another and should be parallel to the blade. Their main purpose is to house the miter gauge, an essential component for making crosscuts. A miter gauge consists of a swiveling, protractor-style head attached to a metal bar that fits in the miter slots. The miter gauge travels in the miter slot, ensuring that workpieces pass straight through the blade. Miter gauges can be adjusted for making 90° cuts as well as mitered crosscuts at any angle down to 30°. Most miter gauges have pre-set stops at 90° and 45°. A graduated scale on the back of the head determines the cutting angle. The best miter

gauges have large heads with scales delineated to single degrees, although even these scales don't guarantee accuracy. The front of the miter gauge head flattens into a short fence for supporting workpieces during the cut. A handle on top locks the miter head angle and keeps your hand clear of the blade.

Many new contractor's and cabinet saws come with a T-square style rip fence (right) that clamps to a single front fence rail. The fence slides on an "L" bracket mounted along the back of the saw table.

Older rip fence styles (below) generally are hollow steel bars that clamp to a pair of tubular fence rails in front and back.

Rip fence & rails. Cutting a board lengthwise and along its grain is called ripping, and a rip fence makes this operation possible. Rip fences are oriented parallel to the blade and can be repositioned along the length of the table for ripping workpieces to various widths. Rip fences usually ride on one or two hollow steel or aluminum tubes, called fence rails, which are located along the front and back of the saw table. Other rail styles include steel "L" brackets or a combination of brackets and tubing. The rails on some benchtop saws are molded right into the tabletop casting.

Rip fence bodies are typically made of hollow steel or extruded aluminum. Better fence designs come faced with slippery high-density plastic surfaces or laminate-covered wood, which make it easier to slide workpieces along the fence as well as attach sacrificial or auxiliary fence jigs. Fences clamp and lock to either the front rail or both the front and back rails during cutting to keep the fence parallel to the saw blade. The front rail has a measurement scale along its length for setting the cutting width, and the fence clamp usually has an adjustable cursor for indexing the fence on the scale. A stout lever on the fence clamp locks and unlocks the fence on the rails.

Not long ago, budget-priced table saws often came with inaccurate, flimsy fences that frequently fell out of alignment with the blade and were difficult to set precisely. A poor fence leads to sloppy cuts, burned edges, and even kickback (see page 80). Fortunately, the construction market and demanding woodworkers have convinced saw manufacturers to improve rip fence quality in recent years. While it's still possible to buy a saw with a poor rip fence, most new saws come with reliable or even highly precise fences that are easy to adjust. If your saw suffers from a low-quality rip fence, you may be able to retrofit it with an aftermarket fence.

Guard & splitter. All table saws are equipped with a plastic or metal blade guard that covers the blade during ripping and crosscutting. A guard protects you from exposure to the blade teeth while helping keep sawdust from blowing up in your face. The guard attaches to a

Rip fences on benchtop saws are becoming more accurate and sturdy as the quality of these saws improves. They often clamp to the front fence rail only.

flat plate of metal called a splitter, positioned immediately behind the blade and about the same thickness as the blade. As its name suggests, the splitter keeps wood on either side of the blade from closing up on the outfeed (back) side of the blade after it is cut. Wet wood or wood that contains internal stresses will often close around the blade during cutting. When this happens, the wood pinches and binds the blade, sometimes to the point that the blade lifts and throws the wood toward you. This hazardous situation is called kickback. Without some form of splitter, there is no other practical or safe way to keep the saw kerf open behind the blade.

Rip fence accuracy and parallelism depend on the sturdiness of the front clamping mechanism. This T-square rip fence clamp provides broad support for holding the fence square and keeping it locked. The measurement scale is easy to read, and the clear cursor window is adjustable to refine the fence settings in relation to the scale.

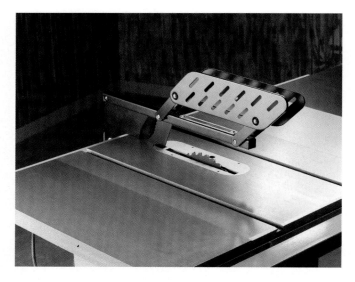

Saw guards and splitters still look largely like they did decades ago. The guard and splitter are a one-piece unit. The metal guard pivots up and down to ride over workpieces while keeping the blade covered.

Most splitters are straddled by a pair of jagged-edged, metal antikickback pawls. The pawls are spring-loaded and allow workpieces to move from the infeed to the outfeed side of the blade, but not in reverse. In the event that wood binds on the back of the blade, the pawls dig into the workpiece and hold it against the table rather than allowing kickback to occur.

Conventional guard and splitter assemblies do a decent job of making sawing safer, but some designs limit your ability to see around the blade during a cut. Splitters fall out of adjustment from time to time and may even hang up workpieces as they pass by the blade. Guards cannot be used for most dadoing and rabbeting operations because these cuts don't cut all the way through the workpiece so it fits around the splitter. Even though rip fences are getting better, guards and splitters still suffer a host of maladies and are often removed and discarded. Sawing without a guard and splitter is inherently dangerous. Fortunately, most full-sized saws can be fitted with first-rate aftermarket guard and splitter assemblies that can be used for all sorts of cutting operations. Some have helpful dust-collection features too (see page 46).

Saw controls. Table saw blades can be raised and lowered as well as tilted. Most saws are equipped with a pair of handwheels for making these blade adjustments, although a few styles provide for both functions with only one handwheel. The front handwheel tilts the blade either left or right, and a side handwheel raises and lowers the blade, depending on the make of saw. Worm gears on the ends of the handwheel shafts mesh with racks of teeth on the arbor assembly or the saw's internal cradle to pivot these parts. A knob in the center of the handwheels locks the settings. Saws have a bevel tilt scale in front to indicate the degree of blade tilt.

Blade controls vary, but most saws have two handwheels—one in front for raising and lowering the blade and another one on the right or left for tilting the blade.

A saw's power switch may be located on the base or the front rail and should be large enough to shut off by simply bumping it with a hand or knee. Many power controls are the "remove-to-lock" style with a pin that pulls out, locking the switch in the off position for safety. If the power switch on your saw is difficult to reach without fumbling for the control, consider moving it out to the front rail or replacing it with a larger switch. You should be able to shut off the saw without looking for the switch in the event of an emergency.

Motor & internal mechanicals. A saw's electric motor will hang either inside the saw base or just behind it on a hinged plate. On contractor's and cabinet saws, power from the motor transfers to the blade by way of automotive-style "V" belts and pulleys mounted on the motor and the saw's arbor shaft. Depending on the size of the saw, there may be one to three pulleys and drive

Blade elevation handwheel

Blade tilt handwheel

POWERMATIC

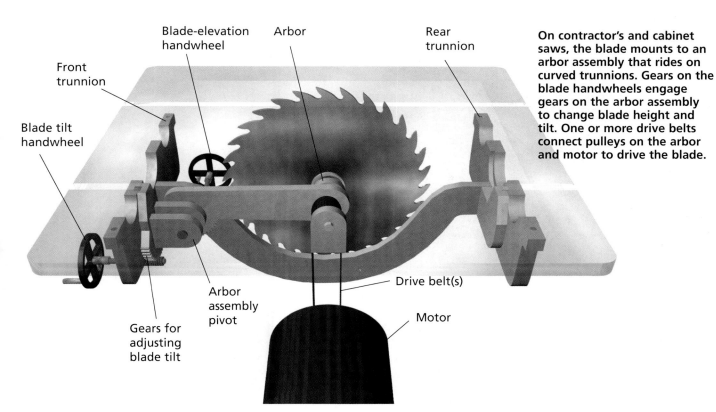

Front trunnion

Blade-elevation handwheel

Arbor

Rear trunnion

Blade tilt handwheel

Gears for adjusting blade tilt

Arbor assembly pivot

Drive belt(s)

Motor

On contractor's and cabinet saws, the blade mounts to an arbor assembly that rides on curved trunnions. Gears on the blade handwheels engage gears on the arbor assembly to change blade height and tilt. One or more drive belts connect pulleys on the arbor and motor to drive the blade.

belts. Conversely, benchtop table saws have no pulleys or belts. On these smaller machines, the motor shaft doubles as the blade arbor, and the blade bolts directly to it.

Mid-sized and larger table saws have semicircular castings called trunnions that support the arbor and related parts. Hanging between the front and back trunnions is an iron cradle with an arbor assembly that swings in an arc to tilt the blade as well as pivot it up and down. The blade arbor, which is simply a machined spindle for attaching the blade, rides on a pair of sealed bearings in the arbor assembly. When the handwheels are turned, the arbor assembly and motor move as a single unit so the drive belts and pulleys remain aligned. On professional-grade saws, the trunnions and arbor assembly are made of cast iron to help dampen vibration and produce smoother cutting.

Refer to your saw owner's manual to acquaint yourself with the internal layout of your machine's trunnion, arbor, and motor. The configuration of these internal components will vary based on the type and model of saw.

Saw base. Saw bases range in shape and size, from floor-standing cabinets that totally enclose the internals to open-backed boxes. Some are made of high-impact plastic, but most are made of steel. The saw base provides a rugged platform for supporting the tabletop and a chamber to help contain or channel sawdust out of the tool. Contractor's saw bases come with metal legs to make them floor-standing, while cabinet saws have bases that stand directly on the floor. Benchtop saws need to rest on a workbench, sawhorses, or other shop-made workstands to bring the saw up to a comfortable working height. Some new hybrid saws are equipped with bases that are a cross between a cabinet and a leg set.

The larger the off switch, the better. This oversized paddle switch makes it easy to shut down the saw with a nudge from a knee or foot as well as by hand. In an emergency, you may not have a hand free to shut down smaller, conventional power switches.

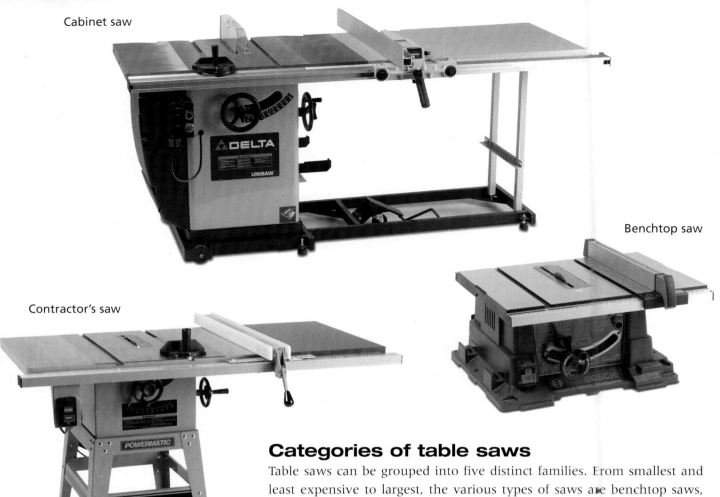

Cabinet saw

Contractor's saw

Benchtop saw

Categories of table saws

Table saws can be grouped into five distinct families. From smallest and least expensive to largest, the various types of saws are benchtop saws, contractor's saws, cabinet saws, and an emerging mix of hybrids and multi-purpose machines.

For a tool that performs a fairly straightforward number of tasks, it's remarkable how many different models and varieties of table saws exist, in a range of prices and levels of quality. Choosing the right saw takes some honest assessment on your part. Your decision should be influenced by several factors, and key among these is saw performance. Think about the range of cutting tasks you typically do now and the kinds of advanced operations you might like to explore in the future. If remodeling jobs and light-duty woodworking are your fare, a lower-priced table saw might be a good fit. Budget-priced machines from any reputable manufacturer are powerful enough to rip and crosscut ¾-inch-thick lumber, especially soft-woods such as pine and cedar. These machines are reasonably accurate. Since slicing up plywood and 2 × 4s for rough construction is less exacting work than making finger joints and tenons for furniture, there's no sense in paying top dollar for accuracy.

On the other hand, if you plan to pursue woodworking as a serious hobby or an eventual vocation, buy a table saw that will grow with you. Furniture building and cabinetry demand more versatility and accuracy from a table saw than making simple rips and crosscuts for remodeling or basic woodworking. Cutting through thick hardwood and spinning dado blade sets or molding heads also requires a saw motor with plenty of muscle. To cut precise furniture joints, you need a saw that holds its tuning, runs smoothly, and allows workpieces to be guided accurately against the rip fence and miter gauge.

To help choose the saw that's right for you, study the following overview of each saw category. In addition to these descriptions, learn more about specific models by reading articles in woodworking magazines. Woodworking editors test the latest machines and give their impressions of quality and value. Some magazines even provide annual buyer's guides that list all the current models of table saws with complete specs and prices so you can comparison shop without ever leaving home. What you can't find in printed form is often available on the Internet. Every major tool manufacturer has a web site. There are scores of woodworking forums and chat groups in cyberspace as well, where you can post questions and talk about table saws with woodworkers of all skill levels. You might also find it helpful to attend national woodworking shows that come to your area. These events provide informative tool demonstrations with experts on hand to answer specific questions. Using this mix of resources, you'll surely find a machine that fits your sawing needs and budget.

If your workshop needs to travel with you from time to time, a benchtop table saw may be the answer. Lightweight components and small proportions make it easy to lift into and out of a trunk or truck bed.

Benchtop saws. If you're an occasional woodworker or looking for a table saw to tackle light- to medium-duty cutting tasks, a benchtop saw might be the perfect machine. These saws could also be the right choice if your "workshop" amounts to what you can carry in a truck bed or fit underneath a workbench. You can tuck a benchtop saw into the same space as a full-sized microwave.

All benchtop saws these days have aluminum tabletops, and most have integrated extension wings. Table dimensions vary, but typically they are about 20 inches deep and 26 inches to 36 inches wide—about a foot shorter in both dimensions than larger saws. Benchtop saws have lighter-duty internal components made of pressed steel or alloy castings instead of iron. Blades mount directly onto the end of the motor's armature shaft, which is threaded to receive an arbor nut. In a sense, this "direct-drive" configuration makes benchtop saws function like inverted circular saws. The handwheels raise and lower or tilt the motor, just like the shoe on a circular saw. The bases on these saws are usually sheet metal or high-impact plastic.

Lightweight components and smaller table dimensions make benchtop saws attractive to contractors

Most benchtop saws have direct-drive transmissions. The motor shaft forms the saw arbor, and the entire motor moves with the blade for changing blade height and tilt. A pressed or cast metal saw carriage holds the motor.

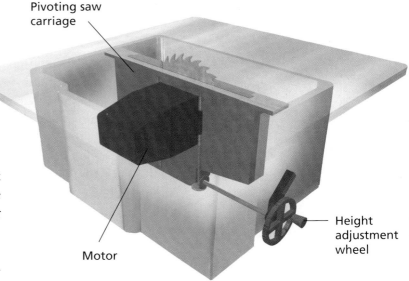

Pivoting saw carriage

Motor

Height adjustment wheel

Collapsible saw bases set benchtop saws to a comfortable working height on the job site. Some are equipped with wheels for rolling the saw where it is needed.

Photo courtesy of DeWALT

who need their saws to be portable. In fact, most benchtop saws weigh just 50 to 75 pounds, so they're easy for most people to lift and carry without help. Motors on these saws are the universal type, just like routers, corded drills, and other handheld power tools. Universal motors take up less space than the larger, heavier induction motors that come with bigger saws, so they fit neatly into small saw bases. These powerplants develop short bursts of respectable horsepower—up to 2 hp in some cases—and draw around 15 amps at the plug. But higher amperage means they can't sustain peak horsepower for long periods of time without overheating. And peak horsepower isn't the same as "rated" or "continuous" horsepower, a more reliable measure of what the motor can deliver for long durations under extreme loads. Universal motors are significantly louder and generate more vibration than induction motors, and they'll live shorter lives between overhauls. Cutting wet-treated or thick-dimension lumber and hardwood will slow down or even stall the blade on these modestly powered saws.

As far as cutting capacities go, nearly all benchtop saws accept standard 10-inch diameter saw blades and offer a 3-inch depth of cut at 90°. Buy a saw with a ⅝-inch diameter arbor. Some benchtops have ½-inch-diameter arbors, which limits your range of blade options to mostly what you can find for use in portable circular saws. Choose a benchtop saw with an arbor that's at least 1¼ inches long so it can accept dado blades as well as standard saw blades. Dado blades greatly increase a saw's versatility. (See page 34 for more information on dado blades.)

Not long ago, most benchtop saws came with low-quality rip fences that were difficult to align and adjust. Miter gauges were outfitted with flimsy, undersized heads and crude protractor scales. Now most benchtop saws come with precision rip fences and improved miter gauges. Other attractive features on pricier saws include rack-and-pinion table extensions that extend the tabletop for wider ripping, left-tilting arbors, and provisions for improved dust collection. Not all benchtop saws have better components, so beware of budget-priced saws, especially those sold by lesser-known tool manufacturers.

If you are shopping for an upper-end benchtop saw, compare the prices of these machines with mid-range contractor's saws. You'll likely discover that the price difference is small. Contractor's saws are becoming more economical all the time, and their quality is hard to beat. A contractor's saw will offer more muscle, capacity, and precision for your tool dollars than any benchtop. But if your saw needs demand that the machine be portable and easy to store, a benchtop saw is still a sensible choice.

Contractor's saws. The next step up in capacity and size is the contractor's saw. Developed during the housing boom of the 1950s, these saws were a portable alternative to the heavier, cast-iron saws of the time. Carpenters could transport a contractor's saw weighing 200-300 pounds much more easily from job site to job site than table saws designed for stationary use.

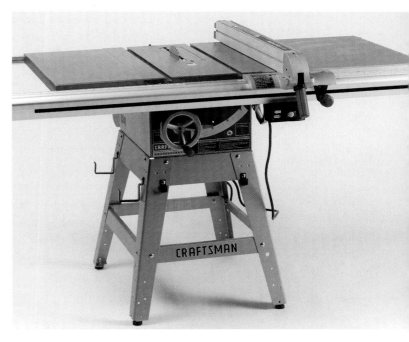

Contractor's saws offer the best combination of features, performance, and quality for the average woodworker. For starters, the saw tables are about the same size as cabinet saws—about 27 inches deep by 40 inches wide. These dimensions provide ample surface area for carrying out most ripping and cross-cutting tasks. Some saws come with side extension tables that increase the maximum ripping width from 24 inches to more than 50 inches. The extra room comes in handy for supporting and cutting full-sized sheets of plywood. Tables are cast iron with steel or iron extension wings. Some iron wings are webbed, but the preferred style is solid. Most contractor's saws come with first-rate rip fences that are easy to keep aligned and require little or no routine tuning. Miter gauges on these saws tend to be much larger and heavier than those on benchtop saws for better workpiece support and improved accuracy.

Contractor's saws offer full-sized proportions and ample power, but are still relatively easy to move around. Their motors are mounted on a pivoting plate behind the saw. Motor weight tensions the belt on the arbor and motor pulleys.

Unlike either benchtop or cabinet saws, which have motors mounted beneath the table, contractor's saw motors hang behind the saw on a hinged plate. One long drive belt extends from the motor to the arbor pulley, and it's kept tensioned by the weight of the motor. Motors are induction style rather than universal, and they range from 1½ to 2 rated hp. Most are the TEFC (totally enclosed, fan cooled) variety, which requires no lubrication or periodic cleaning. These larger motors deliver ample power to drive standard 10-inch saw blades through all types of wood up to around 3⅛ inches thick. They're also well suited for spinning heavier dado blade sets and molding heads. Induction motors are typically wired for regular 115-volt outlets, but they can be rewired fairly easily to 230-volt service, which cuts their amperage draw in half. (See page 44 for more information on rewiring a saw motor.) Motors run cooler and ultimately longer when wired to the higher voltage.

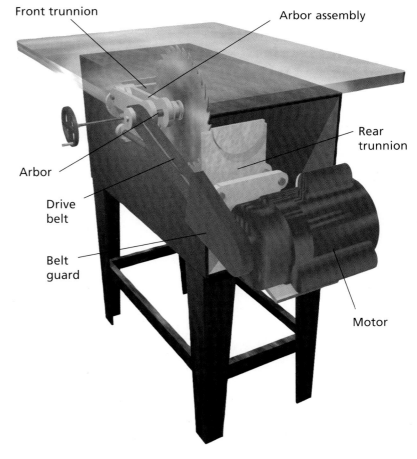

Front trunnion

Arbor assembly

Arbor

Rear trunnion

Drive belt

Belt guard

Motor

Contractor's saws have open bases and legs that place the saw table height at around 34 inches. The open base style and legs help shed some pounds off the machine, but these saws are far too heavy to be called portable. You'll need help to tote one up and down a flight of stairs or lift it into a truck bed. A rolling base makes these saws easy to move into position for cutting and then out of the way for storage—something you'll appreciate if your workshop doubles as a space for parking cars. Some contractor's saws are outfitted with a provision for dust collection, usually a dust port plate that attaches to the bottom of the saw base. Others come with a fabric bag that snaps into place between the legs to catch falling dust. Either way, the back of the base must be covered to make dust collection reasonably effective. Some woodworkers do this by outfitting the back of the saw with a plywood cover.

A new, middle-of-the-road contractor's saw can be had for around $500, which is significantly cheaper than buying a cabinet saw and only a bit more expensive than most benchtop models. There are a host of aftermarket accessories available for contractor's saws, including micro-adjust rip fences, guards and splitters, precision miter gauges, and tenoning jigs, which make these workhorses even more accurate and versatile. Most contractor's saws have arbors that tilt the blade to the right, but some new models now feature left-tilting mechanisms. All this said, contractor's saws are a great value for your tool dollars. If you are more than an occasional woodworker but don't have aspirations beyond a hobby, buy a contractor's saw.

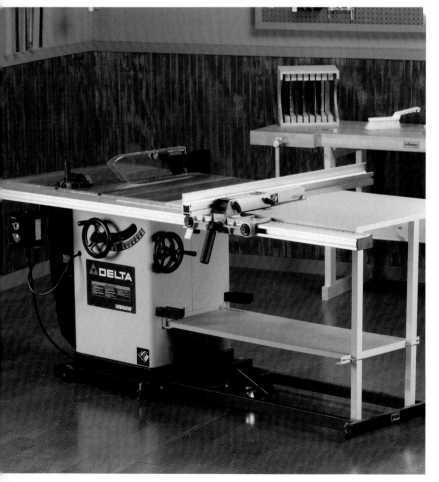

Cabinet saws. Cabinet saws have been the preferred table saws of professional woodworkers for more than a century. While contractor's saws provide solid performance for a fair price, they can't match the precision, reliability, and power offered by these flagships of the table saw family.

Sheer heft is probably the single biggest attribute that sets cabinet saws apart from the rest. Table and extension wings are always made of cast iron, along with truly massive arbor and trunnion assemblies beneath. These parts are made of much thicker metal than in a contractor's saw, and they rest on the saw base for added stability rather than hang from the table. Iron dampens vibrations produced by the motor and pulleys, which transfers straight to the blade and leads to rough cuts. Vibration is

Cabinet saws are heavy but offer rock-solid accuracy and performance. Many models come with long side extension tables for working with large sheet materials. A cabinet saw is moveable, provided it's outfitted with a rolling base, like the one shown here.

also the culprit for wear and tear on bearings, arbor spindles, and pulleys. Reduced vibration helps keep cabinet saws in "tune" longer than their lighter-built counterparts. In fact, once a cabinet saw is tuned up, it may stay that way for many years before needing adjustment.

Cabinet saws are equipped with large, heavy-duty induction motors. Motor sizes range from 2 to 7 hp, and they are capable of producing substantial amounts of torque. Two or three drive belts deliver this power to the arbor. The shorter cabinet saw belts provide more efficient power transfer than the long contractor saw belts. Beefy trunnions and arbor cradles help support the motor's added weight. Stout undercarriage parts prevent the motor and belts from literally twisting the arbor cradle out of alignment, which would skew the blade's orbit.

Cabinet saws come in both right- and left-tilt styles, depending on your preference. You can buy saws that accept 12-, 14- or 16-inch blades, but 10-inch-capacity machines are still the standard woodworking choice. Most of these machines are wired for 230-volt electric service.

Since cabinet saws are aimed at the professional market, they're generally outfitted with precision rip fences, large miter gauges, and sturdy handwheels and controls. A wide variety of aftermarket accessories are available for expanding the capabilities of a cabinet saw. A number of components, such as roller outfeed tables, sliding crosscut tables, and power feed units are specially suited for industrial or production work. You can outfit a cabinet saw with a rolling base

Front trunnion

Cradle

Drive belts

Motor

Rear trunnion

The motor of a cabinet saw mounts below the arbor assembly and drives the arbor by way of two or three short belts. The entire undercarriage of these saws is made from thicker castings than other table saws for improved vibration dampening.

Among a host of aftermarket accessories, cabinet saws can be outfitted with sliding crosscut tables that work like giant miter gauges. These fixtures offer superior crosscutting accuracy and control over large workpieces.

Photo courtesy of Grizzly Industrial, Inc.

A door or hinged cover on a cabinet saw provides access to the motor and undercarriage for routine cleaning and maintenance tasks.

to make it somewhat portable, but moving 500 or more pounds of table saw around the shop is a chore you won't want to do often.

Cabinet saws get their name because the bases are fully enclosed. The undercarriage and motor are accessible through a door in the cabinet or a hinged or removable motor cover. Closed bases provide a rigid platform for the machine and help capture the sawdust. All cabinet saws come with a port or opening on the cabinet for connecting to a dust-collection system. Enclosing the motor also helps the saw run more quietly.

Owning a cabinet saw is a tantalizing thought, especially if you're a woodworker who demands precision and long tool life. A cabinet saw will likely be the last saw you'll ever need to buy, and it may even pass down a generation or two. However, adding one to your shop will set you back at least $800, and twice this amount or more for a professional-grade machine. Add an aftermarket guard or an extension table kit and you'll probably spend an amount equal to a top-shelf contractor's saw plus a couple of other stationary woodworking tools. If you've simply got to have a cabinet saw but your budget isn't limitless, consider buying a used saw (see page 22).

Hybrid saws & multipurpose machines. A new category of hybrid table saws is now emerging to bridge the gap between cabinet and contractor's saws. Essentially, these hybrids look like a cabinet saw from the outside but share some aspects of both cabinet and contractor's saws inside. They also sport a

Multipurpose woodworking machines combine several heavy-duty tools into one compact unit. Most of these machines feature a table saw, shaper, planer, and jointer, each with its own motor. The machines are designed to change over from one tool function to another quickly and efficiently.

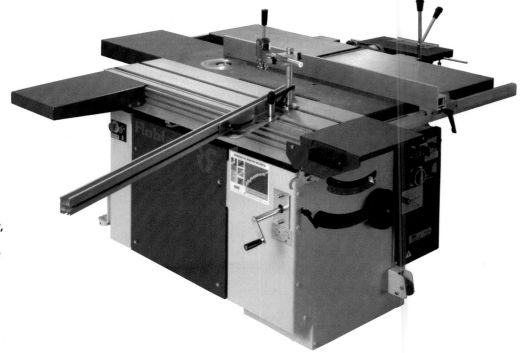

Photo courtesy of Laguna Tools

more affordable price tag. The motor and undercarriage are concealed inside a partial or full cabinet, and the rip fence, miter gauge, and table casting are more robust than you'll find on the average contractor's saw. Inside the base, the motor and cradle configurations loosely resemble a contractor's saw. Motors hang from a pair of steel tubes or from a modified iron cradle and trunnion assembly that bolts to the table. The induction motors on these machines fall in the 1¾ to 2 hp range, so they're a bit larger than many contractor's saw motors, but smaller than a cabinet saw's motor.

Aside from conventional-looking table saws, there are also numerous multipurpose machines that combine several stationary tools into one compact package. Typical multipurpose machines operate as a table saw, jointer, planer, and shaper, with a separate induction motor powering each tool. These machines are manufactured in Europe, where tool quality exceeds what you'll find in mass-produced machinery from China or Taiwan. If you are woodworking in a small shop or have a large tool budget, European multipurpose machines give you the highest degree of precision and maximum versatility without taking up much more room than an ordinary saw with an extension table. Top-quality multipurpose machines have extension tables, sliding crosscut tables, and sophisticated guard and splitter assemblies to further extend the capabilities and safety of these machines. Expect to pay several thousand dollars for these machines used, or many times that amount for one fresh from the crate.

Hybrid table saws are the new kids on the block, blending the lighter weight of contractor's saws with the stouter undercarriages of cabinet saws. Larger motors, improved dust collection, and more standard features are other factors that put these new saws a step ahead of many contractor's saws.

Photo courtesy of DeWALT

If a European multipurpose machine is out of your price range, there are reasonably priced consumer models not made in Europe. These tools have a single heavy-duty induction motor that drives all the different tool functions.

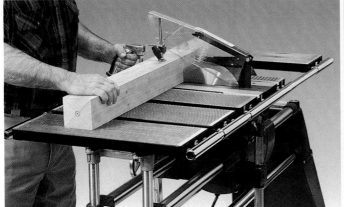

Single-motor multipurpose machines convert from one woodworking function to another, but many of the tools that fit these machines must be purchased as add-ons. A table saw, drill press, lathe, and horizontal borer are standard equipment.

Photos courtesy of Shopsmith Inc.

Usually the motor slides on a pair of tubes to engage the various drive mechanisms of separate tools. You'll get a table saw, lathe, and drill press as standard equipment. The tool can also function as a jointer and band saw, but these features must be purchased separately.

Shopping for a used saw

It's hard to resist the urge to buy new machinery, especially if you're a tool junkie. Any well-made table saw is a significant investment. If your price range is limited, buying a new saw might force you to settle for a lower-quality tool or one that won't meet your needs. Over the long haul, you'll probably forget how great it was to uncrate a new machine when you're struggling to push a board through an undersized or underpowered saw.

One sensible option to keep you from either breaking the bank or settling for less is to buy a used saw. Table saws often can be found in the classifieds section of newspapers or woodworking magazines. You'll run across them at auctions from time to time, especially when manufacturing companies or cabinet shops go out of business. Table saws turn up in garage and estate sales as well. Some larger metropolitan areas have tool stores that take in used machinery as trade-ins or consignments. Internet auction sites list page after page of used table saws, but you'll have to bid and buy without the benefit of trying the machine out beforehand. If you find a used saw you like in cyberspace, be extremely vigilant and ask the seller lots of questions about the machine before you make your bid.

Your area might have a machinery store dedicated to selling new and used woodworking equipment. If new isn't all-important to you, consider shopping for a used saw instead. The savings can be significant without compromising quality.

There's good reason for the prevalence of used contractor's and cabinet saws. Machines built for heavy-duty use can function for decades before they need major servicing or replacement. It's not uncommon for cabinet saws, especially ones that are well maintained, to cut for decades or longer in production situations. Contractor's saws can live a full second or third life with a new set of bearings, a fresh belt, and eventually a motor overhaul.

The longevity of table saws works to your advantage as a used saw buyer. Often, you'll be able to purchase a higher-quality used saw for the same price as a lower-grade new machine. However, there are a number of pitfalls to avoid when shopping for a used saw, as well as several components you should inspect carefully on the saw before you buy. Here's what to look for and keep in mind as you search:

Use a straightedge to check whether the table on a used saw is flat. Don't buy a saw with a warped table, no matter how reasonable the price.

Saw table. Buy a saw with the largest tabletop you can find. There's simply no substitute for having ample working room when you're sawing. Some used saws come souped-up with features such as side extension tables to make the tables more spacious. Cast-iron saw tables offer solid value, provided they are flat and free of cracks and severe pitting. However, don't pass up a saw simply because it has an aluminum tabletop rather than one made of iron. If you have to have a portable saw, an aluminum tabletop might be your only realistic option. Aluminum tabletops must also be flat and free of cracks. Peek up inside the base of a saw with an aluminum tabletop. If the underside of the table has deep ribs in the casting, it's more likely to stay flat than one with a largely smooth casting.

Check the flatness of the tabletop with a reliable 3-foot straightedge. The table should be flat from front to back, side to side, and corner to corner. The entire working surface of the table must be as flat as possible for the tool to produce accurate, square, and flat sawn edges. Be sure the extension wings of the saw meet the tabletop flush where the parts bolt together. The extension wings may tip up or down from the rest of the table or meet unevenly along the joint, but provided you can access the attachment bolts on the wings, they're easy to flatten out (see page 58). Shine a flashlight between the straightedge and the table from behind to see if the table has any dips or humps in the surface. You can correct minor deviations of this sort, provided they don't exceed 1⁄16 inch across the surface of the tabletop. Minor rust can also be removed without much consequence (see page 53).

Inspect the throatplate on a used saw for signs of blade damage. Although this plate has surface rust, the blade slot is still smooth. If it's the original throatplate, the saw has been kept reasonably tuned over time.

Cracks in the table surface are a bad sign. Oftentimes you can't see them easily without a magnifying glass. Cracks usually indicate that a tabletop has suffered some significant trauma. The saw may have tipped over or been dropped in transport. It could be cracked as a result of a misdirected hammer blow if the saw table was used as a workbench or if something heavy fell on it. With iron tables, cracks sometimes indicate that the casting didn't cure properly when it was made, and internal stresses have distorted and fractured it. This isn't common, but it can happen. Whatever the cause of the crack, it's hard to fix a cracked tabletop, and replacing the top can be expensive. You're better off finding another used saw instead.

Miter slots. Inspect the miter slots for signs of wear and tear. Over time, these slots widen slightly as they are slowly worn by the action of the miter gauge. This process takes decades and isn't cause for concern. It's fairly easy to adapt the miter gauge bar so it fits more tightly in the slots (see page 64). Look for burrs as well as excessive rust build-up or pitting along the slots. Usually these kinds of minor damage can be smoothed out or scrubbed clean with a fine-grit sharpening stone, a file, or coarse steel wool.

Throat plate. Have a look at the saw's metal throat plate. It doesn't really matter what the plate's surface finish looks like so long as the saw blade opening is smooth all around. If the opening looks like it's taken a few chops from the blade along the way, you can be sure the machine was badly out of tune at some point. Blades should never make contact with a metal throat plate under normal circumstances. If the saw you're considering has a chewed-up metal throat plate, you're bound to find other signs of neglect or hard use elsewhere on the machine. Even a plastic or shop-made wooden throat plate should have a smooth blade slit. The opening may be enlarged if the blade was set at an angle and passed up through the plate, which is nothing to be concerned about, provided the slot is even and smooth.

Lock the rip fence and attempt to push the rip fence body from side to side or along the rails. A quality rip fence that's properly adjusted should hold its position when the fence clamp is engaged.

Miter gauge & rip fence. While used saws can surpass the quality of some newer machines, older rip fences and miter gauges may fall far short of the mark. Only within the past decade or so have table saw manufacturers begun including precision fences on many consumer-grade contractor's saws. Most older cabinet saws should have adequate fence systems, since these machines have always been built for professional use. Be particularly wary of benchtop saws made prior to 1995, regardless of the manufacturer. Vintage benchtop saws have chronically feeble and unreliable fences.

Here are a few indications of quality in an older fence and miter gauge: Look for large and heavy fence bodies, fence rails, and miter gauge heads. The miter gauge bar should be made of solid metal, not sheet stock formed to fit the miter slots. The miter gauge head should be a steel or iron casting with a large, easy-to-grip locking handle. The protractor scale should be stamped into the miter gauge head and highlighted with bright paint for easy reading.

Test the action of the rip fence's clamp mechanism on the rails. It should lock down firmly and not shift when you apply side-to-side pressure on the fence body. The fence may or may not clamp to the back rail, depending on its design. Either way, a good fence stays put once you set and clamp it. Slide the fence along the full length of its rails. The fence should move smoothly and without binding while remaining parallel to the miter slots. A quick test is to slide the fence up to one of the slots, lock it down, and see how it tracks the slot from front to back. Some deviation here can be corrected by tuning the fence (see page 62) or realigning the table (see page 57). You'll also want a fence system that includes a large cursor and prominent scale markings on the front fence rail for indexing the fence and blade. Many used fences show signs of scoring on the face—an indication that the fence was set too close to the blade for a ripping or joint-making operation. Unless the fence faces are severely scored, minor blade damage isn't a major issue here. You can attach a sacrificial fence face to cover up this kind of damage or replace the face piece to provide a smoother contact surface.

A blade arbor with the belts removed should spin smoothly and silently when you spin it by hand. Any clicking sound or roughness usually indicates that the arbor bearings are worn and need to be replaced.

Rip fences have adjustment screws or bolts so the fence body can be aligned parallel with the blade. These provisions are located on the fence clamp or on top of the fence body. There may also be a bolt situated on the end of the fence for adjusting the clamping pressure on the fence rails. The more adjustment features there are, the better.

If the rest of the saw looks like a good buy, but either the fence or the miter gauge are sub-par, these parts usually can be replaced. A reliable rip fence and miter gauge are crucial to cutting accurately. You'll have to decide how much the saw is actually worth, given that a new fence and rails will cost about $300, and an improved miter gauge $50 to $100 or more.

Internal components. Remove the throat plate and the drive belt cover (on contractor's saws) for a closer look at the internal components. At the same time, pull off the drive belt or belts if you can. On contractor's saws, this step is as easy as lifting the motor a bit and slipping the belt off the motor pulley sheaves. Removing multiple drive belts on a cabinet saw is time consuming, difficult, and probably beyond the scope of your saw inspection. Nor will you earn any brownie points from the saw's owner by asking him or her to do this for you. However, freeing up the arbor and motor drive pulleys can tell you much about the condition of the arbor bearings, the trueness of the arbor spindle, and the general health of the motor.

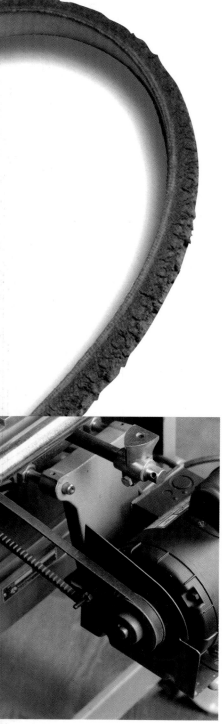

Saw drive belts eventually become glazed, develop cracks, or dry out and crumble, like this one. They're easy and inexpensive to replace.

On a used contractor's saw, pull off the belt guard and inspect the motor pulley sheaves. They should be smooth and polished. This is also a good way to survey the condition of the drive belt.

Bearings & arbor. With the drive belt or belts removed, raise the blade above the table all the way and give it a good spin by hand. The blade should spin silently and in a flat orbit on its axis. Any clicking or grinding you hear indicates that one or both arbor bearings are worn and in need of replacement. Bearings can be replaced relatively cheaply on machines made within the past 50 years, but you'll probably need to have this work done by a machine shop. If the blade wobbles, more than likely the blade is out of true, but it could also indicate that the arbor spindle is bent or the blade flange is damaged. You'll need to test the arbor spindle and flange with a dial indicator (see page 56) to further investigate wobbling. Try installing a different blade to see how it compares with the first. If it also wobbles, there's trouble brewing at the arbor.

Rotate the motor pulley. The motor armature should turn smoothly and without clicking or grinding. Try to move the motor armature shaft in and out of the motor housing. Any noticeable play here indicates worn bearings. Some bearings can be replaced easily and relatively inexpensively, but you could be faced with replacing the entire motor. You can't know which scenario you're facing without having the motor inspected by a machine shop or an electric motor repair service. New saw motors cost about $150 and up, or less if they're reconditioned.

Run a fingertip around the inside surfaces of the pulleys. The sheave walls should be polished smooth and flat. Eventually, pulleys begin to dish out in the sheave area as these surfaces are worn by the belts, but this process takes many years. Some wear and tear here is acceptable, but deeply worn pulleys allow the drive belt or belts to slip under heavy cutting loads. They also cause premature belt wear. Pulleys are replaceable. If you can't obtain them through the saw manufacturer, you can probably buy them from the motor manufacturer or a machinist's supply outlet. Likewise, glazed or cracked drive belts should be replaced before they break. For saws with multiple drive belts, order new belts in "matched sets" so they'll have exactly the same circumference.

Undercarriage. Take note of other undercarriage parts. Inspect the worm gears on the ends of the handwheels for signs of pitting, burrs, or uneven wear on the contact surfaces. These gears are exposed to all the crud thrown off by the blade during sawing, and they'll wear faster than they should unless they are periodically lubricated. The worm gears mesh with teeth on the front trunnion as well as on the arbor cradle for raising and tilting the blade. The trundle and cradle teeth should be evenly shaped. Broken teeth, which are an unlikely occurrence, indicate that something hard was cranked through the gears.

You'll know the worm gears and teeth are in good shape if the handwheels move the blade completely through its range of motion without grinding, thumping, or excess play in the controls. It's important that the undercarriage gears and teeth mesh properly, since they're responsible for keeping the blade from drifting out of position during cutting. Stiff or squeaky handwheels could simply indicate that the mechanism and gears need a good cleaning and lube (see page 53). Another way to test the fitness of these parts is to tighten the lock knobs on the handwheels. If the gears are meshing properly and without excess wear, it should be difficult to turn the handwheels further when they are locked.

Motor. For any saw other than a bench-top model, you'll surely be dealing with a long-lived, quiet induction motor. Check the motor's specifications, which are listed on a sticker or metal plate on the outer motor housing. Be sure the motor is listed as single-phase rather than two- or three-phase. Single-phase motors can operate on either 115- or 230-volt household current, but two- and three-phase motors require industrial electric service. Vintage table saws that take blades larger than 10 inches are likely to have two- and three-phase motors. It's possible to run these motors off of household current if they are used in conjunction with a device called a phase converter, but converters are expensive and generally not worth the hassle. Multi-phase motors can some-times be replaced with smaller single-phase motors, but the changeover can be difficult if the saw has an unusual motor mount. You may also need to switch to a new motor pulley with a smaller armature hole.

Most late-model contractor's and cabinet saws have a totally enclosed, fan-cooled induction motor, like this one. If you can see the armature and copper windings inside, it's a much older motor.

Another factor to take note of is whether the motor style is TEFC (totally enclosed, fan cooled). TEFC motors are designed so the inner windings, contacts, and bearings are sealed from external sources of dust and grit. If you can peek through ventilation holes in the motor casing and see the copper windings inside, the motor is not TEFC. TEFC motors are preferable to older open styles, but this is not to say an older motor is doomed to a shorter lifespan. Be aware that if your saw has an older motor with exposed bearings and internal parts, it will need to be occasionally blown clean with compressed air. Contaminants such as sawdust and wood pitch make the motor run hotter and foul the bearings.

Inspect the electrical cord plug on the saw. It will resemble an ordinary house-hold three-prong style if the motor is wired for 115-volt outlets. If the two flat prongs are turned horizontally rather than vertically, this indicates the motor is wired for 230-volt service. A qualified electrician can switch the plug style and rewire the leads so the motor matches the electrical service you have in your shop. Or, you may have to add 230-volt service to your shop. It all depends on the horsepower and amperage rating of the motor. Anything over 2 hp will need 230-volt service.

With the belts connected to the saw and the guards in place, turn on the saw. The motor should start promptly and reach full speed without hesitating. The motor should produce an even-sounding pitch at full speed. Try a few test cuts if you can. Under a normal cutting load and with a sharp blade, the motor should not surge, bog down excessively, or stall. If it does, especially if it also emits a burning smell or smoke, you'll know the motor needs help. Of course, expect the motor to slow somewhat as you push wood through the blade.

Other issues & inspections. If a used saw's table, rip fence and miter gauge, innards, pulleys, and motor appear to be in good condition, you can be reasonably sure the machine has been well cared for and presents a good buy. Other general inspection areas are just plain common sense. Be sure the machine isn't missing any obvious fasteners and comes with a guard and splitter. Check the power cord to make sure it isn't cracked or frayed. If the saw has a rolling base, try to negotiate it into the sale. You'll probably want one in the end. Finally, see if the seller has the original owner's manual for the tool. The manual's schematic drawings and part number listings are invaluable if you should need to replace any components. If there's no manual, you can probably obtain one from the manufacturer.

Selecting saw blades

No matter what type of table saw you own, its cutting performance will only improve by using a sharp, clean blade that's appropriate for the material and type of cut. Despite all the improvements and added features going into today's new table saws, they typically still come packaged with an inferior blade. If you've just bought a new saw and it includes a blade with steel teeth, consider buying a better blade right from the start. The factory blade is probably the weakest link in your new saw's "chain." It won't be suitable for all cutting tasks, and the steel teeth will lose their sharpness in a hurry. In contrast, a fresh, carbide-tipped blade will require less energy from the saw to cut cleanly. Carbide teeth hold their edges exponentially longer than steel teeth. With the right carbide-tipped blade, you might even be able to take your just-cut workpieces straight through to assembly and glue-up without further refinement.

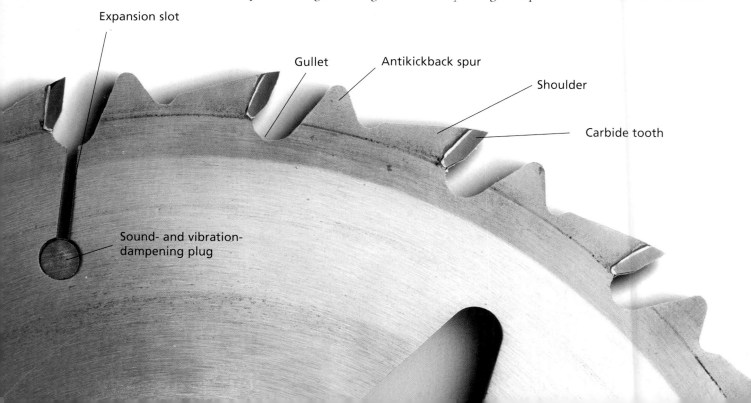

Expansion slot

Gullet

Antikickback spur

Shoulder

Carbide tooth

Sound- and vibration-dampening plug

Choosing the right blade for your saw can be a bit daunting. There are numerous blade manufacturers, each offering a full line of different blades. You'll notice that blades vary in the number, configuration, and shape of the teeth. Some are labeled as "all-purpose" or combination blades, while others are designed for making rips or crosscuts only. Blades may be marketed for cutting specific kinds of materials such as melamine or plastic. If these issues aren't dizzying enough, you have other decisions to make, such as whether to buy a blade with special non-stick coatings or antikickback spurs. Do you need a "thin-kerf" blade, a hollow-ground style, or one that comes with blade stiffening disks? There are literally dozens and dozens of blades to choose from in a wide range of prices. How do you choose?

First of all, you can breathe a little easier knowing that the blitz of blades and styles can be boiled down to a few practical options for most cutting tasks. If you have a jointer for cleaning up your saw cuts, choosing the "right" blade gets even easier because you can afford to be less fussy about cutting quality. But before throwing discretion to the wind and buying the closest blade on the store shelf, spend some time reading the next few pages to educate yourself on matters of blade anatomy, function, and options. In the end, you'll see that it's not too tough to draw your own conclusions and make some wise blade picks.

Anatomy of a saw blade. The main disk of a saw blade is called the blade body. It is either stamped or cut from a sheet of steel, then heated until it tempers to a certain hardness. At this stage, the basic shape and configuration of the humps and valleys around the blade are already set. The "humps," called shoulders, support the chips of carbide that actually do the cutting. The "valleys" between the shoulders form gullets that shovel dust and chips out of the saw kerf as the teeth create them. The more aggressive the tooth cut, the

Although the difference appears to be minor, the narrower kerf cut by a thin-kerf blade (left) allows the blade to cut more quickly and with less energy from the saw than a regular kerf blade (right).

deeper the gullets need to be. Better quality blades also have curved slits cut down through the base of some of the gullets. These are expansion slots, intended to give the outer rim of the blade room to expand as it heats up without warping the blade body. Some blades also have curved slots or cutouts in the mid-section of the blade, which help dampen vibration and reduce blade noise. A few manufacturers install copper or bronze plugs into the expansion slots to quiet blade noise even more.

It's crucial that blade bodies are flat. The best blades undergo a series of grindings and tensioning in a milling process that ensures they'll be flat. Tensioning involves compressing a narrow ring around the blade to help the blade resist warping. Sometimes you can see the ring, but it also may be milled or polished off the final surface. Manufacturers of the finest saw blades guarantee the

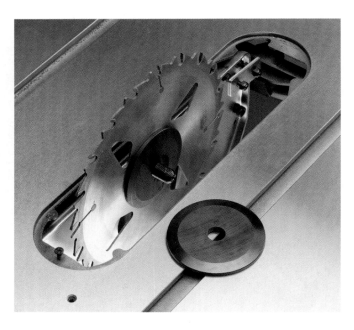

Blade stiffening disks install on either side of thin-kerf blades to reduce deflection and vibration during cutting. The large diameter of the stiffeners reduces the blade's maximum cutting depth.

flatness of their blades in thousandths of an inch. The blade's arbor hole is also carefully positioned, cut, and ground to final diameter. This ensures the blade will spin precisely on center and fit the arbor spindle without play.

Blade bodies vary in thickness, depending on the intended use of the blade. Most are about ⅛ inch thick, but you'll also find "thin kerf" blades that cut narrower ³⁄₃₂ inch kerfs. The thinner blade bodies are more prone to flexing, especially when cutting through thick or damp lumber and hardwood, but they're a good choice for saws with motors having less than 1½ rated hp. The thinner profile requires less energy from the motor. Choose a thin-kerf blade if you own a benchtop saw, though you can use a thin-kerf blade on any table saw for easier cutting.

Some thin-kerf blades come with one or two metal disks that fit next to the blade on the arbor and stiffen it during cutting. Stiffeners do help, but they reduce the blade's maximum depth of cut by about ½ inch.

Once the blade bodies are tensioned and milled, carbide teeth are brazed into pockets in the blade shoulders, ground to the proper shape, and polished until they are razor sharp. Blades with carbide teeth are standard these days, due mostly to the fact that tungsten carbide is 40 to 50 times harder than ordinary blade steel. Carbide teeth hold their edges for years when used occasionally and for normal wood-cutting tasks. Eventually the teeth will chip and break, but this takes a long time, unless you hit a nail or accidentally drop the blade. The teeth will also deteriorate more rapidly if the wood pitch isn't removed occasionally.

Tooth styles & hook angles. Carbide blades come in several tooth configurations. The number, shape, and set of the teeth on the blade determine the different blade styles. Let's start with the shape and set of the teeth. Carbide teeth are ground across the top in three different ways: flat, beveled to a sharp point, or flat and with the top corners nipped off. Flat-topped teeth cut with a chiseling action and leave a square-bottomed kerf. Beveled teeth cut like tiny knife blades with a shearing action. On general-purpose saw blades, beveled teeth are set on the blade in alternating patterns of left- and right-facing bevels, producing a "V"-bottomed kerf. The grind of the bevel angles varies. Steeper grinds allow the teeth to cut more cleanly, but the tips are more fragile. "Triple-chip" teeth have corners chamfered off at 45° angles. They're designed to remove a little less material than flat or beveled teeth. The design keeps brittle materials such as laminates or sheet plastic from chipping during cutting.

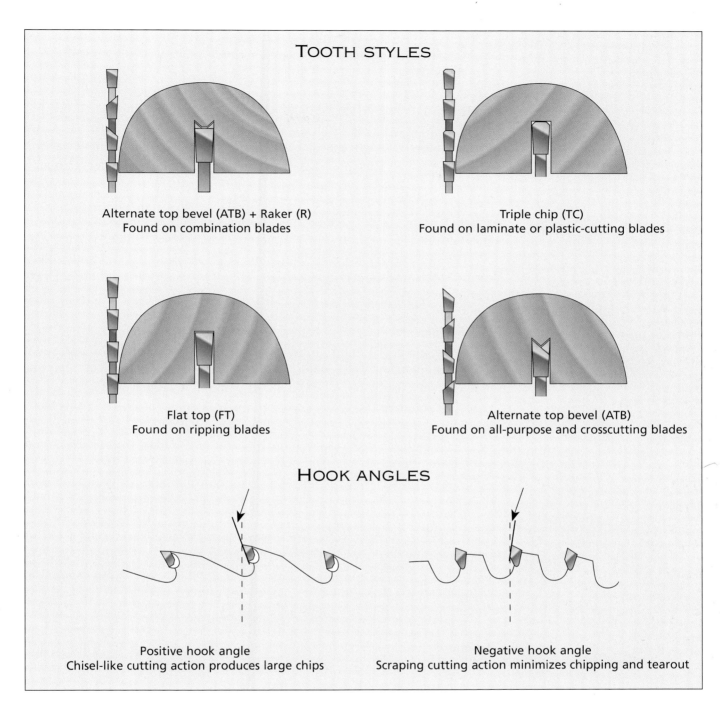

TOOTH STYLES

Alternate top bevel (ATB) + Raker (R)
Found on combination blades

Triple chip (TC)
Found on laminate or plastic-cutting blades

Flat top (FT)
Found on ripping blades

Alternate top bevel (ATB)
Found on all-purpose and crosscutting blades

HOOK ANGLES

Positive hook angle
Chisel-like cutting action produces large chips

Negative hook angle
Scraping cutting action minimizes chipping and tearout

Teeth are set at specific angles on the blade shoulders. They may pitch forward on the shoulders, stand more squarely, or even tip backward slightly. This angle is called hook, and it's determined by extending an imaginary line from the center of the arbor hole out to the face of the teeth. There are numerous degrees of hook angle, engineered to work in harmony with different tooth grinds. Forward-tipping teeth have positive hook, and they'll cut aggressively but less cleanly. Teeth with negative hook have no hook angle or cant back on the shoulders. They cut with a slower, scraping action that produces smoother cut edges and fine sawdust.

Blade styles. Along with grinds and hook angles, teeth are combined in different ways. When only flat-top teeth are used, the configuration is called flat-top grind (FT). Blades with FT teeth are made for ripping wood. Rip blades

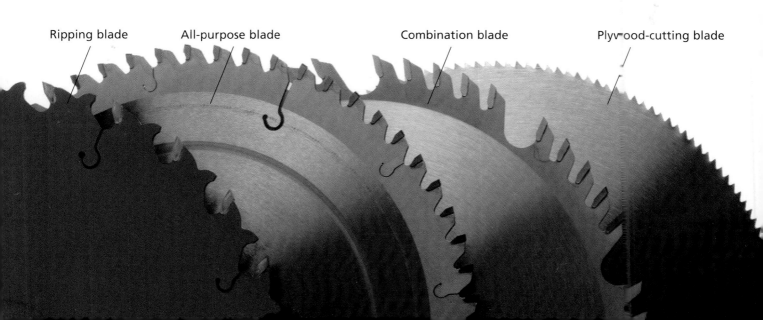

TIP

Blades are sometimes sold in several choices of finish, including chrome or variations of anti-stick coatings. These enhancements can't hurt, but provided you clean your blades periodically, the special finishes won't translate into differences you can "feel" during cutting or possibly even see on the final cut edge. Don't choose a blade on the basis of whether or not it has a special finish.

have only 18 to 24 teeth with deep gullets in between. They cut quickly and cleanly along the grain but make messier crosscuts. The teeth are set with a positive hook angle to enhance their bite.

Blades with only bevel-edged teeth are configured as alternate top bevel grind (ATB) or a variation called high alternate top bevel grind (Hi-ATB). The latter style uses teeth with steeper bevel angles. Teeth on ATB blades have beveled edges alternating right and left. ATB tooth grinds are quite common because the teeth do a decent job of both ripping and crosscutting. These "all-purpose" blades usually have around 40 ATB teeth separated by medium-sized gullets, and they're the current rage for general table saw work. Crosscut blades, which are also called cut-off or finishing blades, have between 60 and 80 smaller ATB teeth and tiny gullets. As their name implies, these blades are designed to slice cleanly across the grain. They're a great choice for miter saw use, but the cutting speed is too slow to be practical for table saws.

Combination blades, another common option, have been around for years. This style combines ATB and flat ground teeth into an effective cutting recipe. You'll know a combination blade when you see one; the teeth are set apart in groups of five—two pairs of left and right bevels with one FT tooth used as a "raker." Combination blades have between 25 and 50 teeth, depending on the blade diameter. Gullets between the beveled teeth are moderately sized, and there's a deep gullet in front of the raker tooth just like a rip blade. These blades offer a good compromise between clean cuts with or across the grain as well as respectable cutting speed. Before the advent of the all-purpose blade, combination blades were the style used extensively for general table saw use.

Blades sold for cutting laminates, plywood, and plastics have ATB teeth or Hi-ATB teeth paired with triple-chip grind (TC) teeth set at a low positive hook angle. Some laminate blades have TC teeth combined with raker teeth. The chamfered teeth are set just a bit higher than the raker teeth to shave the beginning of the kerf, then the rakers pare away the rest of the waste.

Another option for cutting plywood cleanly is to use a blade outfitted with tiny steel teeth rather than carbide. These inexpensive blades have about 200 teeth

Ripping blade All-purpose blade Combination blade Plywood-cutting blade and are a good choice if you cut plywood only occasionally. The small teeth cut slowly, but they do a good job of not splintering the delicate plywood face veneers.

Choosing your blade. With all this blade jargon in mind, what blade or blades do you choose? The issue really boils down to what kinds of cuts you will make most and how much you are willing to spend on your blade arsenal. If you plan to use a table saw primarily as a ripping machine, which is common if you also own a power miter saw for crosscutting, buy a ripping blade. On the other hand, if your table saw will spend equal time ripping and crosscutting a variety of wood and plywood, an all-purpose or combination blade will serve you well. Specialized laminate- or melamine-cutting blades probably aren't worth the added expense, unless you are fabricating cabinets or countertops. A Hi-ATB blade or an all-purpose blade will do a respectable job slicing melamine, laminate, and plywood cleanly.

Whichever route you take, blades come in a range of prices. Expect to pay anywhere from $30 to $150 or more for a single blade. Quality usually improves as the price tag increases. Be aware that budget-priced blades likely come with thinner carbide teeth that may not be sharpenable when the time comes. You'll probably get a thinner blade body, softer carbide particles, poorer tooth brazing, and rougher cutting surfaces on the teeth. But if glass-smooth sawn edges aren't really a concern for you, lower-priced blades may offer decent value. On the flip side, a finely machined but expensive blade can be sharpened many

INSTALLING A SAW BLADE

Saw blades are held in place on the arbor with a large conical washer and nut. The arbor nut threads onto the arbor counterclockwise, against the direction of blade rotation. This ensures that the nut will not loosen as the blade spins. The washer compresses flat against the blade and nut when it's tightened to lock the nut in place.

Changing a blade involves holding the blade stationary and loosening the arbor nut. Some new saws have arbors milled with a pair of flats for gripping them with a wrench. On these machines, blade changes are a two-wrench affair—one on the arbor nut and another holding the arbor. Most table saws do not have provisions on the arbor for holding it steady. You'll have to wedge a piece of scrap wood against the blade teeth to hold it while twisting the nut loose. Or buy a blade removal accessory that covers the blade and holds it still.

When tightening the nut, it isn't necessary to use brute force, provided you are using the arbor nut in tandem with the proper arbor washer. Just tighten the blade until you nearly reach the point where the nut won't turn any further. This way, the nut will be easier to remove next time you need to swap a blade.

times. Your cuts will be smoother overall, and the blade may spin more quietly. Premium blades often cut so cleanly that the edges are ready for glue-up without further jointing or planing.

Dado blades. The primary function of a standard saw blade is to cut a workpiece in two. The dado blade's purpose is to cut only partway through a board, creating a trough. When the trough runs across the grain, the cut is called a dado. The same cut made with the grain makes a groove. Many woodworkers call both cuts dadoes.

Dado blades can also be used to modify the edges of a board, such as when creating rabbets, tongues, or grooves for tongue-and-groove joints (see pages 98 to 129). By varying the width and depth of dado cuts, you can create a multitude of different interlocking wood joints. Dado blades expand the capabilities of a table saw to such a degree that they really shouldn't even be considered an accessory.

Dado blades come in two styles. The first, typically called a stacked dado blade, consists of a pair of carbide-tipped saw blades with beveled teeth facing in one direction. When mounted on the saw arbor, these two blades form the outer edges of the dado cut. The teeth of one blade face right and shear the right wall of the cut, while the other blade's left-facing teeth create the left wall. In between these blades are one to five chipper blades that clear out the remaining waste.

Arrange the outer blades and chippers on a stacked dado blade so the carbide teeth don't touch one another.

These intermediate blades are either cross-shaped or rectangular, with one carbide tooth on the end of each of the blade body projections. Chippers are made in a range of thicknesses from as little as $\frac{1}{16}$ inch up to $\frac{1}{4}$ inch. You'll get a number of different chipper thicknesses when you buy a stacked dado blade. By combining the outer blades with different arrangements of chippers, you can cut dadoes and grooves to any width up to about $\frac{13}{16}$ inch.

Another dado blade style is called a wobble dado. Wobble dadoes have a single blade with flat-top teeth and large gullets. The blade is mounted on a thick hub that holds the blade at an angle. This hub is made of two wedge-shaped parts that rotate in opposite directions to change the pitch of the blade.

As the blade spins, it wobbles back and forth on its axis, creating the cut. The hub is marked with width settings that indicate the approximate size of the dado cut.

Some wobble dado blades have two conventional-looking carbide blades installed on the hub rather than one. The blades have many more teeth than the single-blade style. This style pitches the blades in a "V" configuration. Twisting the hub changes the width of the "V" at the open end, forming a wider or narrower cut.

Dado blades vary in price from less than $50 to more than $200. Stacked dado blades generally are more expensive than wobble dadoes because they have more parts. Since the blades don't cut in skewed relationship but straight into the work, stacked dadoes tend to produce clean, square, flat-bottomed cuts. However, this isn't always the case. If the chippers and blades aren't precisely the same diameter, the cuts will produce stepped or uneven bottoms.

Wobble dadoes can be found for about half the price of a stacked set. Well-engineered wobblers can produce a square-bottomed cut on par with a stacked set, but they're more likely to make dadoes and grooves with sloped bottoms. As the pitch of the blade changes on the hub, cuts become more or less flat along the bottom. Double-blade wobblers may cut uneven bottoms as well, usually dishing out or in.

Most professional woodworkers use stacked dado blades, especially for cutting intricate joinery where the joint parts show. If you plan to use your dado blade for less precise work, a wobbler dado offers significant savings. Regardless of which style you choose, dado blades are sold in 6-, 8- and 10-inch diameters. Choose one that's 2 inches smaller than the recommended blade size for your table saw. Dado blades are heavy and place significant stress on the saw arbor and motor. By using an undersized dado blade, you'll put less strain on the saw. Most dadoing operations only require the top inch or so of cutting depth anyway, so you'll never miss the extra couple of inches you lose by buying the smaller size. Be aware also that some small saws, especially those with motors less than 1½ hp, may not be suitable for dado blade use. Check your owner's manual if you own a small saw.

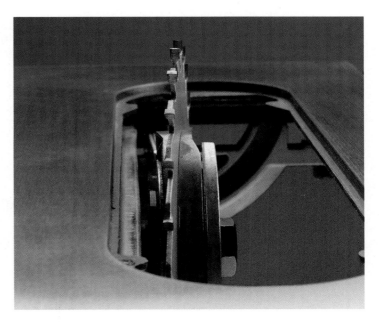

The center hub of a wobble dado pitches the blade on the arbor (below). As the blade spins, the amount of wobble sets the cutting width.

Rotating the hub on a wobble dado changes the cutting width. Notice the demarcations on this hub, which indicate approximate width settings.

INSTALLING A STACKED DADO BLADE

The outermost round blades of a stacked dado blade must be arranged on the arbor so the points of the beveled teeth face away from the chipper teeth. These bevel teeth define the walls and the outer width of the cut. Load the chippers between the outer blades so the chipper teeth fit into the gullet spaces of the outer blades and do not touch other chipper teeth. Stagger the chippers around the arbor evenly to keep the dado well balanced as it spins. Be sure to install an arbor washer next to the nut before you tighten the blade. If there isn't enough room to fit both the washer and the nut on the arbor with all the cutters in place, the dado is too wide for your saw. Take out a few chippers to create some room on the arbor shaft, then make the cut you need in more than one pass.

Molding heads. A molding head can turn your table saw into a shaper. Molding heads consist of a heavy metal hub that spins two to four short steel blades called knives. The knives are sold in matching sets and are sharpened along one edge into various profiles, including coves, grooves, flutes, and beads. Each knife is held in place with a bolt that threads into the hub.

Molding heads have a checkered presence in the woodworking community. Some pros use these devices and recommend them for profiling work. Other woodworkers won't use them at all for safety reasons. The concern is that because molding heads have so few cutters, they take bigger bites of wood. Feeding the wood too quickly or setting the cutting depth too deeply can lead to kickback.

The way to use a molding head safely is to set the cutting height low and make multiple passes, increasing the depth of cut with each pass until you reach the desired profile on your workpiece. Always use a molding head with a zero-clearance throat plate that matches the cutting profile of the knives you are using. Make one the same way you would for ordinary cutting, and slowly raise the molding head knives up through it. The closer the throat plate fits around the cutter opening, the safer the cut will be. (See page 137 for more on setting up a molding head.)

Recently, a new, safer style of molding head has been developed that reduces the kickback hazard. The design employs shoulders behind the knives that limit the amount of material each tooth can remove. This same principle is used with good success to reduce kickback on router bits and shaper knives.

Interchangeable knife sets allow molding heads to cut a host of different profiles for making moldings and trim.

ANTIKICKBACK SPURS

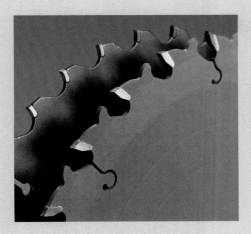

Antikickback spurs are a fairly recent blade innovation intended to limit the amount of wood that saw teeth can remove in each bite. You'll find these devices used on rip and crosscut blades as well as some all-purpose blades. The presence of spurs doesn't slow down the feed rate of the blade much, and they add a margin of safety. If a blade choice comes down to one model with spurs and one without, choose the antikickback style.

STORING BLADES

Invariably you'll end up owning more than one blade for your saw. When storing your blades, keep them separated from one another to protect the brittle carbide teeth from damage. A nail on the wall, a drawer, or a metal shelf are all bad options for storing saw blades. Carbide blade teeth shouldn't come into contact with other carbide teeth or anything harder than wood. Some blades can be stored in their original packaging if it's reusable. An easy shop-made solution is to sandwich each blade between two larger pieces of plywood and run a bolt and nut through the plywood and the blade arbor hole. You can also build a storage box for your blades with dividers inside so each blade has its own compartment. It's fine to arrange the blades on edge in the storage box, provided the box bottom is made of wood or something softer than the carbide. Make the storage box bottom tip backward a few degrees and attach a lip to the front edge. This will keep the blades from accidentally rolling out.

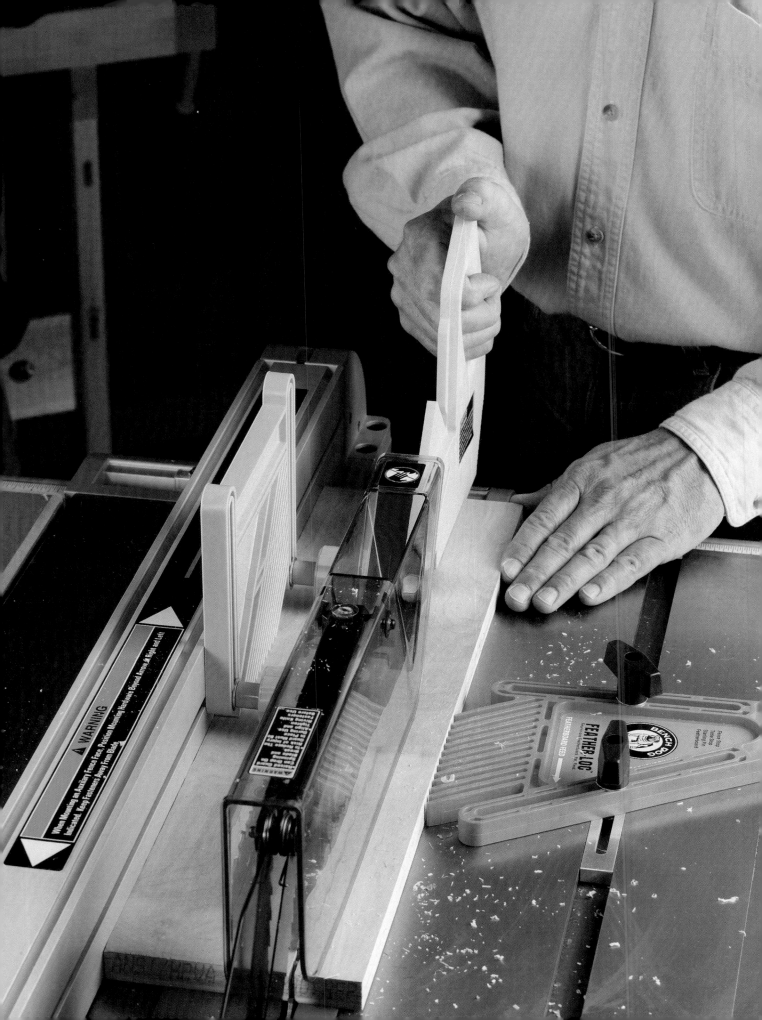

Chapter 2
WORKSHOP SETUP & SAFETY

Workshops are as varied as the people who work in them. In fact, you'll likely spend years perfecting your workspace to suit your particular woodworking interests, budget, and spatial situation. For our purposes, we'll examine those workshop issues that relate to table saws so you can set up your shop for safe, efficient sawing. Familiarize yourself with this chapter, but read other literature on shop setup as well to learn more about setting up your space for other woodworking functions.

We'll begin this chapter by reviewing the kinds of demands a table saw places on your workspace and how to arrange the saw and other machinery to improve the workflow. On a systems level, you'll need to provide the saw with ample electricity, but you'll also want plenty of light overhead so you can see clearly. Some form of dust control will improve the air quality during sawing and keep the floor cleaner. For safety's sake, we'll cover those devices you'll want to have close at hand during sawing as well as what to wear to protect yourself. A number of aftermarket or shop-made implements make a saw easier and safer to use. We'll review several of them in this chapter and others in the chapters to follow.

Space requirements

Machine woodworking is a space-gulping hobby. Ask a dozen woodworkers what they'd most like to improve about their shops, and you'd probably hear a common complaint that the space is never big enough. But even a space as small as a single garage stall or a corner of the basement can serve as a suitable woodshop when you organize it wisely. If you're extremely cramped for space, you might be able to roll the table saw outside when the weather permits and do your large cutting operations there.

Whatever and wherever your space may be, table saws impose a few unavoidable demands on your shop. For one, table sawing requires plenty of clear space around the machine. As a general rule of thumb, you should allot 3 to 4 feet on either side of the saw and 6 to 8 feet to the front and back. A footprint this large makes it possible to rip and crosscut 8-foot board lumber or 4 × 8 foot sheet goods safely. If you don't have this amount of floor space to devote to your saw,

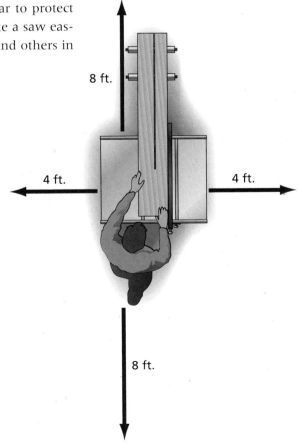

ROLLING SAW BASES

For $150 or less, you can outfit your saw with the single most helpful accessory for cramped workspaces—a rolling saw base. These days a new saw may even come with a rolling base as a standard accessory. Rolling bases may be made entirely of welded steel to fit your particular saw base. There's a rolling base to fit virtually any floor-standing table saw. Or you can buy a kit that comes with metal corner braces that you join together with wooden spars. Wheels make table saws almost effortless to move around the shop. Usually a pair of heavy-duty casters elevate one side of the machine, while a third wheel pivots up and down on a foot pedal to park the saw for cutting.

Another option is to create a shop-made rolling base. A piece of double-thick ¾-inch plywood makes a good platform to bolt to the saw base. Outfit it with four sturdy swiveling casters, and have two of the casters equipped with brake mechanisms. If you are using a benchtop table saw, you can build a cabinet on your sawbase for storing blades, pushsticks, and other accessories right under the saw.

one way to create more room is to lower your workbench so it is just below table saw height. This way, the bench can do double-duty as workpiece support for the saw. Another option is to mount as many of your machines as possible on casters so you can wheel them out of the way to clear the space you need. Of course, not all cutting operations require a huge footprint of open floor, but make sure you have enough room to maneuver workpieces completely through the saw before you actually carry out the cutting task.

Table saws create clouds of fine dust, particularly when cutting materials such as medium-density fiberboard. They also whine like a jet engine with certain blades installed. If you're just beginning to set up a shop in your home, think carefully about dust and noise issues before choosing your basement as a shop site. Basement shops have the benefit of being climate-controlled, but the sawdust and noise will migrate upstairs in no time. The mess will also end up in your laundry if the washer and dryer are located in the basement. Be wary of sawing in the basement if your furnace or water heater has a pilot light. Fine sawdust has a low flashpoint and could burst into flame if it reaches these fuel-

This metal rolling base has two fixed wheels and a third wheel that swivels and locks. This rolling base is sized to fit a specific saw base.

burning appliances. In temperate climates, garages or sheds often make better shops than basements. You'll avoid the hassle of hauling machinery, lumber, and finished projects up and down the basement stairs, and the house stays cleaner. Even if your summer and winter conditions are extreme, you can make a garage shop more tolerable by using space heaters, window air conditioners, and fans.

Organization for efficient workflow

You'll be a more productive woodworker if you can arrange the machinery to process wood in a logical way. Typically, lumber is processed in a series of steps that goes like this: crosscut the board to rough length; joint and plane the surfaces smooth, square, and to thickness; rip the board to final width; then crosscut to final length. If you don't own a power miter saw or radial arm saw, all the crosscutting and ripping can happen on the table saw. Parts may need to go back to the jointer to clean up the sawn edges, then return to the saw for additional joint-making steps.

Try to store your lumber near the entry door so you don't have to carry it through the shop. Keep board lumber close to the radial arm saw or miter saw for crosscutting boards to rough length. Some woodworkers mount lumber racks above or below these machines for convenience. Stage the jointer and planer between the lumber rack and the table saw, and put the saw near the center of the room. Generally a table saw will be your shop's central workstation. Even if you can't leave the machine in one place all the time, you'll find yourself moving it to the center of the room for large cutting tasks. If your saw doesn't have a large extension table attached to it, keep the workbench or other worktable close to the saw for staging parts as you cut them.

Saws create scraps almost as fast as they create sawdust. Have a dedicated scrap bin near the saw for saving all those offcuts you'll want to use later on, as well as a trash can for tossing scraps that are too short to be useful. Keep scraps off the floor or they'll become tripping hazards.

Lighting

Next to bench space and outlets, there's probably no limit to the amount of useful light you can add to your shop. Insufficient overhead light produces shadows, which make it harder to cut accurately and safely. If you use indirect fluorescent lighting, mount the lights directly above the saw and other machinery. Incandescent lightbulbs produce more focused beams of light that can produce glares off the saw table if they are mounted over the saw. Place them just ahead and to the sides of the saw. This placement also keeps your body from creating shadows while you are sawing.

Some rolling saw bases are sold as do-it-yourself kits. You supply the wooden spars and size the base to fit your saw. Metal corner braces hold the spars together. Notice the flip-down third wheel and foot pedal.

A well organized shop has a logical ordering of machinery, with the table saw placed in the center. The work flow of this shop starts at the radial-arm saw; then proceeds to the jointer, planer, and table saw; and ends at the workbench. Lumber is stored conveniently near the door.

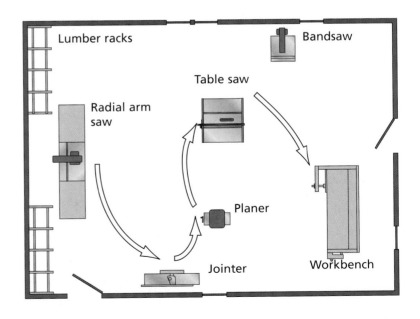

Lumber racks • Bandsaw • Table saw • Radial arm saw • Planer • Jointer • Workbench

Fluorescent tube lighting provides energy-saving illumination. You can buy the 4-foot "shop light" fixtures for less than $10 each. They come with a length of power cord for plugging into an outlet and sometimes a pull chain for turning the lights on and off. Be aware that these bargain-priced fluorescent fixtures have low-quality ballasts that make an annoying buzz when they operate. They can also take forever to warm up in a garage on a cold day, leaving you with dim or flickering light. Better fixtures have industrial or electronic ballasts and deflectors to direct the light downward. For large ceilings, you may want to invest in 8-foot fixtures and hard-wire them directly to a circuit with a wall switch. They're more expensive than economy shop lights, but these long fixtures are made for constant use and come with much better ballasts.

Incandescent fixtures make decent workshop lighting as well, but you'll need more of them to create a balanced amount of light around the shop. The bulbs won't last as long as fluorescent tubes, either. Incandescents and halogen lights really excel in the workshop when they're used as task lighting rather than general ceiling lights. Another option is to use both fluorescent tube lighting and incandescent bulbs. Blending the light sources creates a warmer, more natural light spectrum for your eyes.

Sunlight arguably provides the best general shop lighting. Once you figure a way to get it beaming into the shop, you can't beat the kilowatt price. A skylight or two on the ceiling as well as a few windows or an open garage door could largely replace your need for artificial light during the day.

Electrical requirements

Both universal and induction table saw motors need plenty of electricity to operate at full capacity. Saw motors draw 12 to 18 amperes at the plug under a heavy cutting load. Check your owner's manual or the specifications sticker on the motor housing to see how many amps your saw needs. Induction motors often list two numbers next to the amperage rating, such as "18/9." The first number represents maximum amp draw when the motor is wired for 115 volts. The second figure is half the first, and it indicates the amps required for 230-volt operation. Induction motors can be wired for either voltage. Usually the saw is wired for 115-volt household outlet current for convenience.

It's important that your saw can draw as many amps as it needs to meet your cutting demands. The motor will run cooler, and some experts argue that motors last longer if they aren't routinely starved for power. If the lights dim when you turn on your saw, it's a sign that the circuit is overloaded. The first time you run a thick piece of lumber through a saw on an overloaded circuit, you'll likely blow a fuse or trip a circuit breaker.

Fluorescent lights (top) shed indirect light, so they can be mounted directly over the saw. Incandescent lights (above) should be mounted in front and to the sides of the saw to eliminate glare and shadows.

Assess how many other fixtures or tools are plugged into the same circuit as your table saw. If you have no option but to use this circuit for running the saw, be sure to turn off or unplug other power drains on the circuit to free up as much amperage for the saw as possible. If the circuit still trips, check the size of the breaker in your home's service panel. It will likely be a 15-amp breaker, which is too small for any saw that develops 1 hp or more. Have a licensed electrician wire one or more 20-amp circuits in your shop for operating the saw and other large tools. Run your table saw off a separate circuit from the one that controls the shop lights. Otherwise, a tripped breaker will leave you in the dark with the blade still spinning, and you may not be able to see it.

Never plug a table saw into an ungrounded outlet or remove the grounding pole on the plug. Most saws are almost entirely metal, and any short in the wiring could turn you into the path of least resistance for electricity. Use a neon circuit tester to check the outlet you'll be using for the table saw to be sure it has a working ground. Just because an outlet is three-slotted doesn't mean the grounding pole is properly wired.

You'll probably need to use an extension cord for operating your saw in the middle of the shop. Choose one rated to carry at least the maximum amperage required by the saw. The cord sheathing will usually indicate how many amps the cord can safely carry. The more amperage the cord can handle, the better. Pick the shortest length cord that will work, which will help eliminate a condition called "voltage drop." Voltage drop happens when undersized or particularly long cords create resistance for electricity to pass, starving the motor of power. The cord should be long enough, however, to lie on the floor rather than be suspended in mid-air where it becomes a tripping hazard. If you need to use an extension cord for extended periods, tape it down to the floor.

Your home service panel shows the circuits servicing your workshop. You'll want at least one 20-amp circuit for operating your table saw. Ideally, have a second 20-amp circuit for powering general shop outlets and a third 15-amp circuit for lighting.

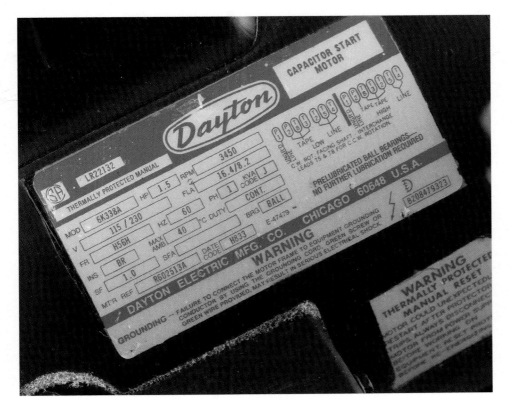

The specification sticker on the motor housing lists the saw's amperage requirements. When wired at 115 volts, this motor draws 16.4 amps. If wired for 230 volts, it draws half the amperage, or 8.2. Lower amperage creates less heat build-up, which extends motor life.

CONVERTING A SAW TO 230-VOLT POWER

Most saws with induction motors can be rewired to run on 230-volt circuits, provided your shop has these receptacles. The switchover isn't terribly difficult. In fact, your owner's manual may supply you with instructions for reconfiguring the plug wires. There may also be a wiring schematic inside the little box where the power cord enters the motor, or the drawing could be printed right on the motor capacity label.

In any case, the process involves converting both the neutral (white) and hot (black) leads of the 115-volt plug wire to two hot leads by attaching them to two hot poles on the motor. In this arrangement, the cord's ground wire then becomes both a ground and the neutral pole, completing the necessary electrical loop. It's entirely safe to use the same 115-volt power cord for this changeover, provided the motor can be switched to 230 volts. (Benchtop saws with universal motors cannot be converted to 230-volt power.) The power cord delivers two sources of 115 volts, or 230 volts total. Neither hot wire has to deliver the full amount of current, which would be unsafe.

Along with the terminal changes inside the motor, you'll also have to splice on a new plug at the other end of the cord. A 230-volt plug still has three metal prongs, but the usual vertical orientation of the 115-volt hot and neutral prongs will switch to horizontal or one horizontal and one vertical. The different arrangement of these two prongs safeguards you from accidentally plugging a 115-volt plug into a 230-volt outlet. Another option is to replace the entire cord with a new cord and prewired 230-volt plug. You may be able to buy this as an accessory from the saw manufacturer or from an electric motor supplier.

Choose the shortest extension cord with the largest gauge wire you can find for powering your saw. A cord with 12- or even 10-gauge wire will provide ample current for any home shop table saw. The maximum safe amperage for the cord is specified either on the cord sheathing or on a label.

Essential accessories

To saw safely and comfortably, you need a few accessories. We've already mentioned rolling saw bases, but other essentials include one or more workpiece support devices, dust collection, and pushsticks and featherboards. You may want to invest in a crosscut sled or sliding miter table for cutting oversized workpieces more easily and accurately. Personal safety gear is a must. You'll need ear and eye protection whenever you saw, and a respirator can be helpful while cutting materials that produce lots of dust or if you're sawing for extended periods of time.

Workpiece support. Ripping and crosscutting operations often involve sizing down workpieces that are much longer or wider than the saw table. To make these cuts safely and accurately, you'll need to set up additional support surfaces behind or alongside the saw. Extra workpiece support is particularly helpful just after you've made your cut and you've got two pieces to contend with rather than one. You should never have to lean over the blade or place your hands or arms in harm's way to steer, support, or catch the wood as it leaves the saw. Support devices alleviate these dangers, and they also keep workpieces from falling off the saw and becoming damaged.

Cabinet shops often have table saws surrounded on three sides with large tables. This way, cutting up sheets of plywood never becomes a wrestling match with gravity.

Roller stands are the typical form of workpiece support for table saws. They consist of a folding metal frame with a roller tube or a number of captured ball bearings on top. Roller stands can be positioned beside the saw for crosscutting wide work or in back of the saw for long rip cuts. The ball-bearing style is particularly useful and less prone to moving because the bearings are non-directional. Be sure the stand you buy can be adjusted up and down and takes a broad stance on the floor. Both types of stand should be weighted down at the base to keep them from shifting or rocking during use.

Roller stands are only one option for workpiece support. Any flat stable surface can help hold up your workpiece during sawing. You could build a worktable just lower than your saw table height and use it for other tasks when it isn't being used for workpiece support. A sawhorse also works if you clamp a taller bearing surface to it. Or simply ask someone to hold the workpieces as they leave the saw.

If you have a cabinet saw, you can buy outfeed roller tables that mount on the saw and fold down when not in use. These are handy but quite expensive. If you're mechanically inclined, you can probably fabricate your own outfeed roller tables or roller stands without much difficulty.

Roller stands provide quick, convenient workpiece support behind or alongside the saw. Most roller stands adjust up and down to suit different saw heights.

Worktables and sawhorses make ideal sidefeed and outfeed table saw supports. Their height should be slightly lower than the saw table to keep workpieces from accidentally hanging up during cutting.

Cabinet saws can be outfitted with outfeed roller tables that attach directly to the saw. The table flips down when necessary to save space.

Dust collection & respirators. Most new saws come with provisions for connecting them to a dust collector. Contractor's saws are more difficult to set up for dust collection than benchtop and cabinet saws. The open design of the base doesn't serve as an effective chamber for capturing the dust. Many saws come with a dust port plate that covers the bottom of the saw and connects to a dust collector, but you'll probably have to cover the back of the saw base as well with a piece of plywood. Cut the plywood to fit around the drive belt housing and motor mount. Attach this plate with screws or bolts so it can be removed when you need to perform routine maintenance.

It's worth the effort and expense to attach your saw to either a large-capacity shop vacuum or a dedicated dust collector. It takes a shop vacuum that draws about 350 cubic feet per minute (cfm) to keep up with a table saw.

Particle filters are available in disposable mask styles or with replaceable filters. Be sure to use one that's approved for filtering out wood dust.

A dust collector port can be attached to the underside of your contractor's saw. The port is then connected to a dust collector.

Although a big shop vacuum will work as a dust collector for a table saw, eventually you should invest in a dedicated dust collector with a 4-inch-diameter hose. Shop vacuums aren't designed to be used as dust collectors for machinery, and no vacuum can keep up with surface planers or lathes that produce heavier chips and shavings. A small dust collector draws about 650 cfm and can service any machine in your workshop, provided the ductwork or hose isn't so long that it impedes suction. You can buy one for about the same price as a large shop vacuum.

Dust collectors are designed in two styles: single-stage and two-stage. Single-stage collectors draw all the dust and chips past an impeller and blow them into a fabric bag. An upper bag traps fine dust as the exhaust air passes through. Two-stage collectors pull debris through a bag or a canister before the impeller, and the larger chips are trapped here first. Fine dust passes through the impeller and into a second collection bag. The advantage of a two-stage dust collector is that there's less wear-and-tear on the impeller over time.

Smaller dust collectors are almost entirely the single-stage variety with one hose port. Larger collectors can be hooked up to two hoses at a time. Both styles can be connected to a branched ductwork system, but the collector should draw more than 650 cfm. Ductwork allows you to leave the collector in one place while still having dust collection wherever you need it in the shop.

Dust collectors won't trap all the fine particles of wood dust floating in the air. To catch these particles, you can mount an ambient air cleaner in your shop. These accessories use disposable or washable filters to trap dust. They can filter all the air in your shop several times an hour if you have a small workspace. Otherwise, wear a disposable dust respirator or a mask with replaceable filters. The verdict is still out on how hazardous wood dust

Dust collectors connected to ductwork systems can collect dust and wood chips anywhere in the shop.

is to your lungs, but research indicates that wood dust may be carcinogenic over time. It makes breathing uncomfortable at the very least. Some wood species such as cedar contain oils that are especially irritating if you have allergies.

No matter what measures you take to control sawdust, open windows and doors to provide fresh air, and use a fan to help circulate the air.

Crosscut sleds & sliding miter tables. There are a few ways to improve the capabilities of a miter gauge, but it's still a small bearing surface for crosscutting long boards, wide panels, and sections of sheet material. A better way to crosscut big panels and long boards is to set them on a crosscut sled or sliding miter table instead. A crosscut sled is essentially a panel of sheet material with two strips attached beneath that ride in the miter slots. The strips keep the panel aligned with the blade, just like a miter gauge. During use, the saw blade passes completely through the sled in a kerf that's cut the first time the sled is fitted for the saw. It also has a fence mounted along the back edge and a brace in front to hold the sled panels together.

Better crosscut sleds have a see-through guard that shields the blade and rises up and down to fit over workpieces of different thicknesses. Some sled designs also come with mitering attachments. Plans for building crosscut sleds are widely available in woodworking project books and magazine articles. Or you can buy manufactured crosscut sleds from woodworking supply catalogs.

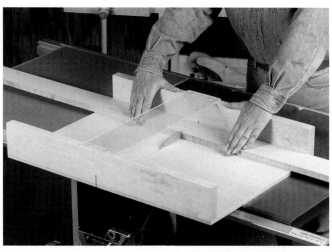

Shop-made crosscut sleds slide over the saw table and hold long or wide workpieces stationary for cutting. They offer improved control over using the miter gauge.

A sliding miter table provides a more stable, accurate way to cut angles than a standard miter gauge with a tiny fence. This one has a hold-down clamp as well.

Another crosscutting accessory you might consider for your saw is a sliding miter table. Most sliding miter table designs replace one of the saw table extension wings and slide on ball bearings alongside the saw table. The table will have a large, adjustable fence for setting angled cuts, just like a miter gauge. Since the gauge is oversized, the protractor scale is larger, which makes it easier to set angle cuts precisely. The table holds workpieces stationary during cutting, sometimes in tandem with a hold-down clamp.

Pushsticks & featherboards. Whether you are using the rip fence or the miter gauge to make a cut, it's critical to keep workpieces held firmly against the saw table and the appropriate fence. Pushsticks allow you to feed workpieces into the blade under firm holding pressure while keeping your hands and fingers clear. Whenever the rip fence is set closer than 6 inches to the blade, use a push stick to guide the workpiece between the fence and the blade. You can buy plastic or wood pushsticks inexpensively or make them yourself from

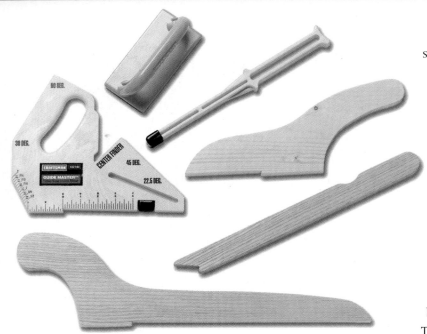

scrap. Either way, they'll eventually get chewed up by the blade. Keep a couple pushsticks within arm's reach of the saw at all times, and replace them as needed.

There's no "best" pushstick design for all applications. Make yours so they are easy to grasp and keep your hands 6 inches or more from the blade. Even a simple "bird's mouth" notch cut in the end of a scrap stick of lumber makes a pushstick. Build at least one pushstick with a longer, flat sole and a tab on the back for supporting wider stock. You can use ¾-inch-thick lumber for making pushsticks, but make a few from thinner ¼-inch material. Thin pushsticks are handy when making rip cuts narrower than 1 inch.

Pushsticks and pushpads for feeding workpieces through the blade can be purchased in many shapes and sizes. Or make your own from scrap. Pushsticks should have a comfortable handle and a notch along the bottom for holding workpieces securely. Pushpads (top in photo) have foam rubber bottoms for gripping workpieces.

Another option for pushing wood through the blade is to use pushpads. These are usually made of plastic with a piece of soft foam rubber fixed to the bottom. You'll find them sold as accessories for jointers, but they work well at the table saw when it isn't convenient to catch a pushstick over the end of a workpiece.

Featherboards hold workpieces against the saw table and rip fence without the need for hand pressure. They're commonly used to make rip cuts or for dadoing operations. A series of springy, narrow wood or plastic "feathers" hold workpieces snugly against the saw table or the rip fence. The feathers are set at an angle so workpieces can be fed into the saw, but they resist the blade's rotational forces that would force the wood back out of the cut. Featherboards are easy to make on the bandsaw by cutting a series of closely spaced kerfs into the edge of a piece of mitered scrap wood. To use shop-made featherboards, clamp them to the rip fence or saw table.

Featherboards hold workpieces against the saw table or rip fence so you can keep your fingers a safe distance from the blade.

If you buy featherboards rather than make them, they usually come with a mechanism that pressure-fits into the miter slots instead of clamping. Some have a metal hold-down tongue to press workpieces firmly down as well as against the fence. Other featherboard styles hold in place with a powerful magnet.

Ear & eye protection. Sawdust is irritating to get in your eyes, and it can lead to a dangerous distraction during a cut. Larger splinters can damage your eyes permanently. Dust and splinters are the usual culprits for eye injuries at the table saw, but so are carbide chips and blade teeth. You can avoid these injuries by wearing a pair of comfortable safety glasses. Spend a little more to buy a pair that are scratch, fog, and static resistant. They should protect your eyes from all sides. Ordinary prescription eyeglasses are not safety glasses, no matter what type of lens they have. You can buy over-sized safety glasses to fit around your eyeglasses, if need be, or even have your prescription lenses fitted for safety glass frames. Buy a neck strap for your safety eyewear, and keep the glasses around your neck whenever you're in the shop. They're a good idea for almost all woodworking tasks.

Table saws produce high-frequency blade noise that can damage your hearing over time. Saws produce around 100 decibels of noise, and anything more than 85 decibels is unsafe. Power saws, routers, planers, and shop vacs can damage your hearing, too.

There are three options for hearing protection: ear muffs, foam inserts, and ear bands. Choose the style most comfortable for you. Ear muffs and bands are easy to slip on and off. Foam inserts are inexpensive and fit right into your ear canals, but the feel takes a little getting used to. Be sure the style you choose is rated to reduce high-frequency noise by 25 decibels or more. Replace them at the first sign of deterioration.

Wear approved ear and eye protection when using a table saw. Your hearing and eyesight could depend on it.

Other apparel for safer sawing. Comfortable rubber-soled athletic shoes provide good traction on slippery sawdust and provide some cushioning if you have a concrete shop floor. You may want to wear a shop apron to keep your clothes cleaner, but do not stow loose items in the apron pockets during sawing. They could slip out when you bend over the saw and end up in the blade. Long-sleeved shirts or a light coat may be necessary in cooler months. Roll up loose sleeves when working at the saw to keep them out of harm's way. Do not wear gloves when using a table saw. Your hands come closer to the blade than any other body part, and gloves can get caught in the blade. If the shop is cold enough for gloves, warm up the space with a heater to make shop time more comfortable.

First aid. Create a safety area in the shop where you can get to it easily in the event of an accident. Mount a first-aid kit on the wall that contains provisions such as gauze, bandages, and a tourniquet, for treating lacerations, puncture wounds, and eye injuries. Install a phone in the shop or make it a practice to carry your cordless or cell phone with you. Program the phone with a few speed dial numbers and keep the phone close by in the event you need to make an emergency call. Hang a fire extinguisher near the first aid kit. Buy one rated for both chemical and electrical fires.

Try not to work in the shop when no one else is home if you can avoid it. Someone should be aware that you are working with machinery and check on you from time to time while you work.

Make sure to include a first-aid area in your shop that includes a first-aid kit, a fire extinguisher, and a phone.

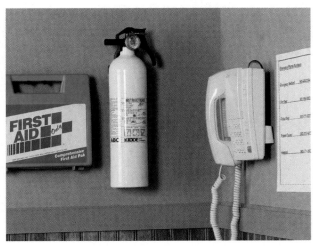

Chapter 3
TUNE YOUR SAW LIKE A PRO

A well-tuned table saw should produce cuts that are nearly ready for assembly or finishing with just a bit of jointing or sanding. Accuracy is particularly important if you plan to use the saw to cut joinery, where a few hundredths of an inch can make all the difference in how two workpieces fit together. Without a careful tune-up from time to time and some maintenance tasks performed on a regular basis, a saw will cut poorly at best and be hazardous to use at worst. All table saws need regular cleanings and a bit of tuning now and then to keep them running in tiptop shape.

Treat this chapter like an addendum to your saw owner's manual. It's ironic that most manuals give you just enough information to put the pieces together, but they don't teach you how to tune up the machine. Most manuals also fail to tell you what to inspect or adjust when problems occur down the road.

To these ends, we'll start with a thorough overview of what to adjust and clean on your saw, along with a list of tools to gather for this work. If you're tuning up a brand-new saw or one you've just acquired used, follow the order of operations as they're listed here. Tweaking one part of the saw often affects other related components, so the order of events is fairly important. On the other hand, if the saw you currently use is beginning to malfunction in a particular way but otherwise seems to be working normally, you might be able to skip ahead in the chapter to troubleshoot and fix the problem without carrying out a full tune-up.

When to tune

Table saws can operate for years without much tinkering, especially cabinet saws or machines that get used infrequently. If your saw is cutting accurately and runs smoothly, a tune-up can be as simple as vacuuming out the interior, lubricating the moving parts, and waxing the tabletop. But chances are you're reading this chapter because something is wrong with your saw right now. If you can answer yes to any of the following scenarios, it's time for some tuning:

TUNE-UP TOOLS

1. 3- or 4-foot straightedge
2. Combination square
3. Dial indicator with a magnetic base
4. Drafting triangle (45°)
5. Flat file
6. Dead-blow or rubber mallet
7. Screwdrivers
8. Socket wrench set
9. Combination wrenches
10. Flashlight
11. Allen wrenches
12. Fine-grit oilstone or water stone

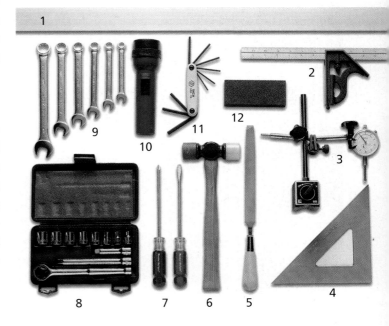

- You are setting up a brand-new saw. (No table saw is thoroughly tuned at the factory. Even those parts that you don't have to assemble yourself may not be properly aligned. Get the machine off to a good start with a careful tune-up.)

- You've just bought a used saw and you are unfamiliar with its history. (Consider any used saw to be in need of a tune-up unless the previous owner tuned it for you.)

- The saw is scorching wood or leaving excessive blade marks during ripping or crosscutting operations.

- It seems harder to push the material along the fence.

- The saw fails to make square crosscuts or rips workpieces with non-parallel edges.

- The handwheels are binding or creaking, and the blade is difficult to raise or lower smoothly.

- The blade will not tilt all the way to 45° or 90° without stopping short, or it exceeds these angles when tilted all the way to stops.

- The rip fence binds on the rails or will not hold position when it's locked in place.

- The saw vibrates excessively during operation.

- You've just experienced a kickback situation or other mishap (the saw tipped over, a blade lost a tooth or teeth, a component of the saw has come loose or fallen off the machine).

When setting up a new saw, oftentimes the tabletop will come coated with shipping grease and protective paper. Remove the paper and clean off the table with mineral spirits.

If your saw is burning the wood when it cuts or leaving excessive blade swirls, it's time for a tune-up.

Tune-up procedure

Clean & lubricate the machine. New saws come partially disassembled. Follow the procedure outlined in your owner's manual to assemble the tool. The unpainted cast iron parts may come coated with grease to keep them from rusting during shipment. Before you assemble the machine, clean off the grease with mineral spirits or a silicone spray lubricant. Use a synthetic scrub pad or sponge to clean off the heavy grease. It's important to remove these petroleum-based lubricants before using the saw because they'll attract sawdust and grime. If there is grease applied to the trunnion and handwheel gears, clean it off as well. Sawdust and wood pitch will mix with the grease and compact into a stiff paste that makes the gears difficult to mesh.

In place of the grease, wipe a dollop of automotive or furniture paste wax onto the trunnion and worm gears. Wind the wheels through their full range of motion to distribute the wax evenly, then wipe away the blobs that squeeze out. A thin layer of lubricant is all you need here. You can also use Teflon-based spray or powdered graphite instead of wax.

For used saws, start the cleaning by vacuuming out the saw base interior or blowing it clean with compressed air. Blow out the motor housing as well if it has ventilation slots on the outside. Use a brass- or plastic-bristled brush (an old toothbrush works great) and mineral spirits to remove caked-on sawdust and pitch from the handwheel worm gears and trunnion gear teeth. Sometimes it helps to soak these parts with mineral spirits first. Allow the solvent to penetrate the crud, then brush it away. Once the interior is clean, lubricate the trunnion and worm gears with wax. Use Teflon spray to lubricate the bushings where the handwheels mount on the saw base.

If there is rust on the tabletop or fence rails, or in the miter slots, remove it with naval jelly and #0000 steel wool or a synthetic scrub pad. Scour off

Apply a thin layer of paste wax to the curved trunnion surfaces and worm gears when assembling a new table saw. Wax any other moving parts that are not bearings. Do not use grease, or it will attract sawdust and grit.

Use a straightedge to align the rims of the motor and arbor pulleys so the belt can travel along a smooth, straight path (left).

If the motor pulley meets the straightedge at an angle, loosen the motor mount bolts and shift the motor to align the pulley (right). Retighten the mounting bolts.

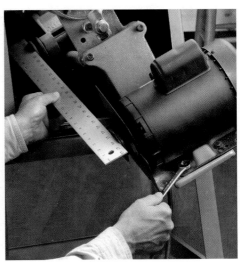

stubborn rust with 600-grit wet/dry sandpaper if necessary. When these surfaces are clean, seal them with a coat of wax (without a silicone additive) to keep them from rusting further. A slippery-smooth tabletop and fence rails make it easier to feed workpieces through the blade and improve the action of the rip fence.

Inspect the drive pulleys for rust, and clean them up, too. Usually the inner sheave surfaces are polished smooth and shiny by the drive belts unless the saw has been stored in a damp place and not used. Cleaning the pulley sheaves promotes even belt wear when you begin to use the machine

As far as other lubrication is concerned, the arbor bearings are typically sealed and permanently lubricated. Apply grease only if there are fittings near the bearings. Inspect the motor housing for information about oiling, and follow the instructions using the proper machine oil. Most newer motors have sealed bearings that are lubricated for the life of the bearings.

Use oven cleaner or a citrus-based cleaner and steel wool or a scrub pad to clean your saw blades (below). Routinely inspect used blades for chipped, cracked, or missing carbide teeth (bottom).

With the saw clean, lubricated, and waxed, give the blade a good cleaning. You'll need a clean, flat blade for adjusting the alignment of the miter slots and arbor. A variety of specialized blade cleaners are sold, but spray-on oven cleaner dissolves wood pitch and sawdust deposits just as well. Citrus-based liquid cleaner also works, and without the caustic fumes. Coat the blade with cleaner in a shallow tray. If you use oven cleaner, seal the blade for a few hours in a plastic bag so the fumes can contribute to the cleaning process. Then scrub the blade thoroughly with fine steel wood or a scrub pad. Don't leave oven cleaner on a carbide blade for extended periods of time. The chemicals can weaken the carbide. Be sure to wear solvent-safe gloves and eye protection.

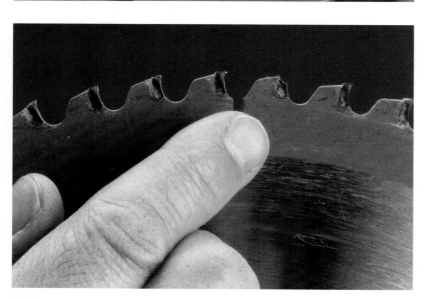

Once the blade is clean and dry, inspect the carbide teeth closely for chipped edges. A magnifying glass makes this process easier. It will also reveal whether there are small cracks in the brazing behind the teeth. If just a few teeth are slightly chipped, the blade is still usable as is. Chipping is a normal part of blade wear, and the carbide will chip sooner if it isn't kept clean. However, if the blade is missing even one carbide tooth or you discover cracked brazings, it's time to send the blade to a sharpening service or replace it.

LINK BELTS

One way to ensure a smoother running contractor's saw is to replace the automotive-style drive belt with a link belt. Link belts are usually colored red and consist of interlocking rubber segments. Oftentimes you'll buy link belts by the foot from woodworking supply catalogs—they can be used just as easily on other machinery, such as drill presses. Link belts form a tighter grip around the pulley sheaves than V belts, and they last just as long or longer. If you can order machined pulleys along with the link belt, it may be worth your while to invest in new pulleys, too. Sometimes the pulleys that come standard on economy saws are cast rather than machined, and they may not spin in a flat orbit or evenly on their axes. Machined pulleys are manufactured to higher tolerances so they'll spin smoothly.

Lay the metal rule of a combination square across the blade body (be sure not to rest it on the carbide teeth) and hold the blade and rule up to a light to check for warpage. There should be no slivers of light appearing between the rule and the blade body. Rotate the blade and check it with the rule all around. Warped blades should be replaced.

Inspect the drive train. With the internal areas of the saw clean, and belts and blade installed, start the machine. A table saw with a properly aligned drive train—motor, belts, pulleys, and arbor assembly—should come up to speed smoothly and run with minimal vibration. Vibration is the worst on contractor's saws because the motor hangs cantilever-style behind the arbor assembly on a hinged plate. If the belt is misaligned between the motor and arbor pulleys, it won't ride evenly and the motor will bounce up and down. It doesn't help that contractor's saws also have single, long drive belts that are prone to more slipping and lash than the short, well-supported belts on cabinet saws. Direct-drive benchtop and cabinet saws are less prone to motor vibration since the motors in these saws are more securely mounted beneath the table. If a benchtop saw vibrates, the source is likely a problem inside the motor itself, such as bad bearings. Cabinet saws generally aren't plagued with much vibration, given their heft, but deteriorated belts or poor bearings are still causes for unnecessary vibration. On any caliber saw, vibration can also emanate from the blade if it isn't spinning in a flat orbit on the arbor.

Vibration migrates out to the rim of the saw blade, causing it to flex back and forth. This action widens the blade kerf and makes rougher sawn edges. A saw that shakes can also cause cut-offs near the blade to drift back into the teeth and be thrown from the tool—usually in your direction. Rattles and jitters make a table saw noisy and unpleasant to use. For all these reasons, vibration is worth remedying during a tune-up.

If blades seem to vibrate excessively, the problem may be as simple as a dirty arbor flange. Clean off any accumulated wood pitch with mineral spirits. Use a soft-bristled scrub brush, if necessary.

Since vibration is a common problem with contractor's saws, we'll use it as the model system for correcting vibration problems. Investigate the alignment of the drive belt and pulleys first. Lay a long straightedge against the outside rims of the motor and arbor pulleys. The pulleys should meet flush with the straightedge. If they don't, loosen the Allen screw that holds the motor pulley on the armature shaft and slide it in or out to see if this brings the pulleys into alignment, then retighten the screw. If the motor pulley contacts the straightedge at an angle rather than flush, loosen three of the four motor mounting bolts and pivot the motor on the hinged plate to correct the problem. Make sure the motor mounting bolts all have lock washers beneath the nuts. Add some if they're missing. Tighten all the fasteners.

Investigate the drive belt (or belts on a cabinet saw) for signs of wear. Worn belts may have glazed, shiny spots on the tapered faces, and chunks of missing rubber or cracks. Minor cracks don't indicate that a belt needs to be replaced, but do replace belts that seem stiff and dry. Buy a new belt if it's missing rubber. When you order belts, be sure to check the belt size in the owner's manual to find the exact replacement. NOTE: On cabinet saws with multiple drive belts, replace all the belts at once, even if only one is damaged. They can be difficult to remove, so you'll save yourself effort later on by replacing all the belts now. Drive belts should have exactly the same circumference, which won't be the case if you pair up one or two new belts with several old ones. Be sure to ask for a "matched set" of belts, which means the belts were cut sequentially from the same blank at the factory.

If aligning the pulleys doesn't eliminate vibration, other culprits are the arbor, arbor flange, or the blade. When any of these items wobble as they spin, the deviation is called runout. You'll need a dial indicator outfitted with a magnetic base to check for runout. First, remove the throat plate, blade, and drive belt. Rotate the arbor and

Excessive runout leads to rough cuts and increased vibration. Use a dial indicator to measure runout at both the arbor flange (top) and the blade (above).

listen for clicking or grinding. It should revolve smoothly and without noise. Grasp the arbor at the flange and attempt to pull it in and out as well as up and down. There should be no play here. Any noise or play indicates that one or more of the bearings are bad. You'll need to remove the arbor assembly and have the bearings pressed out and replaced by a machinist. Usually this work can be done for a reasonable price.

If the arbor bearings seem sound, clean the arbor flange (the large rim surrounding the threaded end of the arbor) and inspect it closely for nicks or burrs.

File any burrs away. The blade must rest flat against the flange or it will wobble. Test for arbor flange runout by clamping the indicator base to the saw table and orienting the instrument down into the throat plate hole. Position the contact point of the indicator on the rim of the flange and rotate the dial's face until the pointer reads "0." Turn the arbor slowly by hand, and take note of the highest numeric reading shown on the dial—this determines the flange runout. If the flange measures more than .003 runout, have it turned flat at a machine shop or replace the arbor spindle altogether.

Install the blade and determine its runout in the same fashion, with the dial's contact arm touching the blade rim just below the gullets. Blades are more prone to warping and deflection than arbors. It's rare to find one that's perfectly flat. In any case, runout should not be greater than .010 for a standard 10-inch blade. Replace a blade with excessive runout. For thin-kerf blades, you can also sandwich the blade between a pair of blade stiffeners to flatten its orbit (see page 30).

Flatten the tabletop. For your blade to cut perpendicular edges, it must meet a perfectly flat saw table at 90°. We'll examine the table for flatness first and make those fixes, followed by any necessary blade adjustments.

Cast-iron saw tables are ground flat at the factory, but they may not be flat when you assemble the machine. This is because the casting needs to season properly (up to about a year) to relieve internal stresses before it is ground flat and smooth. Not all manufacturers wait that long. Check your saw table for warpage by positioning the machine on a flat floor and evaluating the table surface with winding sticks. Winding sticks are simply two strips of hardwood about 20 inches long with flat, smooth edges. Place the winding sticks along opposite edges of the center saw table and stoop down until your line of sight is even with the top edge of the closest stick and about 1 foot away. Look past the front edge of the closest winding stick to the front edge of the other stick. If the top edges of the sticks are even, the table is free of significant twist in this direction. Now place the sticks along the other two edges of the saw table and inspect for warpage again. If the winding sticks are clearly not

Test the saw table to make sure it's perfectly level by placing winding sticks on the table top and sighting across the tops of the sticks at table level (top). Use a long level or other straightedge to check that the extension wings are flush with the saw table (above).

Flatten humps and smooth nicks in the tabletop using a fine-grit sharpening stone and oil or water. Remove just enough metal to flatten the area.

parallel on a new saw, return the machine. You may be able to have a tabletop ground flat at a machine shop if you're tuning a used saw, but be prepared for a potentially expensive fix.

Even if a tabletop isn't warped, it may still dip or rise slightly out of flat here or there, and these areas are easier to fix. Check for low spots by dragging a straightedge across the tabletop lengthwise, widthwise, and diagonally. Shine a flashlight behind the straightedge as you go, and watch for slivers of light to appear. Note the high spots by circling them with a marker or grease pencil. Then grind away the metal in high areas by rubbing with a fine-grit sharpening stone and a bit of water or oil, depending on the stone. Work the iron or aluminum table surface just enough to flatten it out. Use this same method if your saw table has nicks, to keep raised metal from scratching your workpieces. Recheck your flattening efforts frequently with the straightedge.

With the center table inspected for warp and flattened as necessary, turn your attention to the extension wings. These should be flat in relation to the center table so large workpieces will rest flush and meet the blade squarely. Hold a long straightedge against the table lengthwise so it crosses the extension wing joints, and check for flatness with a flashlight. If cast-iron wings aren't flat, they tend to sag down from the saw table along the outside edge. Steel wings might tip up or down. With either type of wing, first check the joints where the wings meet the table. If these aren't flush, loosen the extension wing mounting bolts a bit and tap the wings up or down with a rubber or dead-blow mallet. Also check that the front and back edges of the wings line up with the front and back table edges. Tap them flush, then tighten up the mounting bolts.

If steel wings tip up or down even when the joints are flush, bend them carefully by pressing up or down until they line up with the center table. Cast-iron wings won't flex like pressed steel. If they sag or tip up, loosen the mounting bolts enough to create a gap where the wings attach, and insert a couple strips of aluminum soda can about ¼ inch into the gaps either above or below the wings, depending on which way you want the wings to move. Tighten the mounting bolts and recheck for flatness. Use multiple shims, if necessary. Trim the shims flush with a sharp chisel.

The last tabletop tune-up involves bringing the throat plate flush with the table. What's most important here is to be sure the infeed end of the throat plate doesn't catch workpieces when you feed them into the blade. Use a shorter straightedge held across the throat plate to see how it aligns with the surrounding table. Most throat plates have four Allen screws threaded into them to provide for plate leveling. Turn the screws in or out until no slivers of light are evident

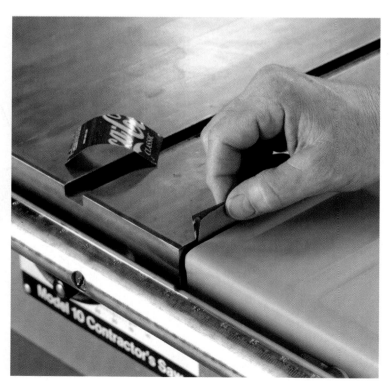

Use strips of aluminum can as shims to raise or lower extension wings that tip up or down from the saw table when tightened in place. Shim on top to drop a wing down, and insert shims underneath if the wing droops.

Zero-clearance throat plates

An easy way to reduce tearout on your cut edges is to replace the metal throat plate that comes with the saw with an aftermarket throat plate or one you make yourself. The advantage here is that you can create a much narrower blade slit in the plate than you'll get on the stock throat plate. In fact, it will match the kerf width of the saw blade. This way, workpieces are supported right up to the blade so they won't splinter when they're cut.

To make your own plate, start with a piece of hardwood that's larger than the metal throat plate and planed to the same thickness as the throat plate recess in the tabletop (often ½ inch). Medium-density fiberboard or cabinet-grade plywood also make good throat plate stock. Use the metal throat plate from the saw as a template to trace the shape onto your wood blank. Cut the throat plate to rough size with a jig saw or on a band saw, then adhere the metal original to your shop-made plate with double-sided carpet tape or clamp the two together on your workbench. Trim the new plate to exact size with a router and piloted flush-trim bit. Guide the bit's bearing against the edge of the metal plate. Check the fit of your shop-made plate in the saw table, and sand the edges if necessary.

To cut the blade slot, crank the saw blade down as far as it will go and set your new plate in the table opening. If the blade makes contact with the plate at this point, switch to a smaller diameter blade that cuts the same kerf width as your standard blade. You can also rout a shallow groove into the bottom face of the throat plate that aligns with the blade to provide some extra clearance for your larger diameter blade.

Hold the throat plate tight against the table with a board and a pair of clamps. Then start the saw and slowly raise the blade up through the new throat plate to cut the kerf. Continue to raise the blade until it reaches full height to complete the blade slot.

Make zero-clearance throat plates for dado blades, molding heads, and those instances when you tilt your standard saw blade to common angles, such as 45°. Be sure to keep the factory original throat plate for use in a pinch or as a permanent template for making more throat plates. It's phenomenal how much cleaner your blade will cut using these inexpensive throat plate enhancements.

Cut a piece of hardwood or plywood to form a zero-clearance throat plate (left). Cut an oversized blank, and use a router and flush-trim bit to trim the blank to match your saw's throat plate. Cut the blade kerf through the throat plate by clamping the new throat plate in place and raising the saw blade until it reaches full height (below).

Use a combination square set against a straightedge and piece of scrap wood to check the blade's alignment to the miter slots. The scrap wood should fit snugly in the miter slot, and the straightedge should rest against the blade body. If the measurements in front and at back of the saw table are not the same, the blade is heeling relative to the miter slots.

between the throat plate and the tabletop. Drag the straightedge across the full throat plate to check that it is flush in all directions.

Aligning the blade with the miter slots. For accurate and safe cutting, the blade must be parallel with the miter slots as well as with the rip fence. When the blade skews out of parallel, the condition is called blade heel. A heeling blade produces scorched edges and causes workpieces to wander away from the fence when you rip them. It makes crosscutting and mitering difficult as well. It's also a dangerous invitation for kickback. (See the opposite page for more on blade heel.)

You can adjust a rip fence so it's parallel to the saw blade, but that won't guarantee that either the rip fence or blade are parallel to the miter slots. A better method is to align the blade and miter slots first, then adjust the rip fence to the miter slots. This way, the blade and rip fence end up parallel with one another. The process for aligning the blade and miter slots involves shifting the entire saw table (on cabinet saws) or the arbor assembly (on contractor's saws) one way or the other until the blade and miter slots align. Doing this may seem cumbersome and nitpicky, but even $\frac{1}{32}$ inch of adjustment will produce smoother, easier cutting with fewer burn marks. Plus, it's a tune-up procedure you'll probably need to make only once or rarely over the life of the machine.

Here's how to check if your blade is heeling relative to the miter slots: Find a strip of hardwood that's about 1½ inches wide, 3 feet long, and fits snugly into the miter slots. The wood strip serves as a raised indicator for the miter slot positions. Set the strip into the miter slot you use most often—typically this is the one to the left of the blade if the blade tilts right, or the right slot for left-tilting saws. Crank the blade up to full height, and check that it's set to 90° using a combination or try square. Lay a reliably flat 3-foot straightedge against the blade body—not the carbide teeth. Lay a combination square on the saw

To eliminate blade heel, loosen three of the four bolts that mount the arbor and trunnion assembly to the underside of a contractor's saw (right), or three of four bolts securing the saw table to the base on a cabinet saw (far right). Shift the sub-assembly or tabletop, retest for blade heel, then retighten the bolts.

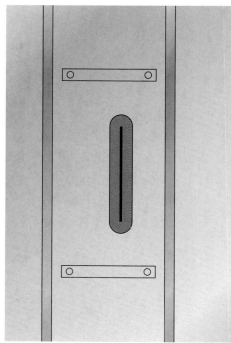

table so its head is against the same reference edge on the straightedge as the blade. Position the square near the front of the saw table. Now extend the rule on the square until it touches the wooden strip, and lock the rule at this measurement. Be careful not to jar the straightedge away from the blade as you do this. Then shift the square to the back of the saw table and position it against the straightedge again. With the square's rule still locked in place, does the end of the rule touch the wooden strip here? If the rule comes up short or pushes the square's head off the straightedge, you'll know the blade is heeling further from or closer to the miter slots. If you are lucky enough to have the rule just touch the wooden strip, skip the following procedure.

If you're adjusting a cabinet saw, locate the four bolts that secure the saw table to the base, and loosen three of the four. On contractor's saws, find the four bolts that mount the arbor and trunnion assembly to the underside of the saw table. Loosen three of these bolts. Pivot the table of your cabinet saw or tap the trunnions of your contractor's saw to shift these components, and recheck the alignment of the blade and miter slots. Use the combination square and wooden strip method to check your progress. Remember that the amount you need to shift the table or arbor assembly is probably miniscule, so work gently. A tap or two with a rubber mallet or dead-blow hammer may be all it takes. When you're making the adjustment on a contractor's saw, it's tough to tap the trunnion assembly if you're working inside the saw base from below. Use a wood block and rap down through the throat plate opening instead, or work from behind the saw. When the blade and miter slots line up, retighten the mounting bolts.

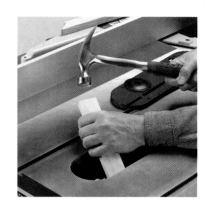

With the mounting bolts loosened, tap the trunnion assembly on a contractor's saw through the throat plate opening using a block of wood and a hammer. This will shift the blade arbor in relation to the miter slots.

TWO TYPES OF BLADE HEEL

A blade can heel in two ways: on the infeed side so the leading edge of the blade is closer to the fence, or on the outfeed side where the back of the blade is closer to the fence. Either way, the blade will cut at an angle to workpieces during both ripping and crosscutting. In fact, it will actually cut workpieces twice as the blade rises out of the saw table on the back edge and spins down into the table on the front edge.

Double-cutting heats up the blade, which eventually begins to burn the wood.

Blade heel is especially problematic for making rip cuts. When the blade heels on the infeed side, it acts like a wedge, pulling workpieces away from the fence. Outfeed heeling turns the blade into a funnel with the fence. The funnel narrows as workpieces pass by the blade and bind against the blade teeth in back. This situation will cause kickback if the rear blade teeth grab the wood and propel it forward over the blade.

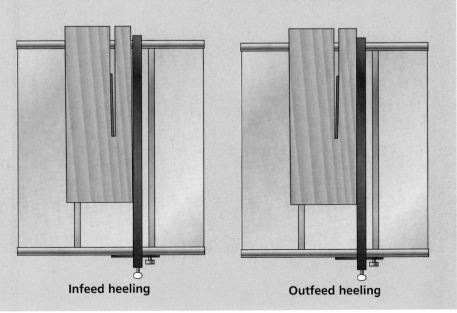

Infeed heeling   **Outfeed heeling**

Aligning the rip fence. Now that your blade is parallel to the miter slots, you can eliminate all sources of heeling by adjusting the rip fence so it's also parallel to the miter slots. Fence designs vary in terms of where the adjustment bolts or screws are located. Older fences have two bolts on top of the fence body, while newer fences may have adjustment screws on the outside of the fence or on the big clamp that holds the fence on the front rail. Check your owner's manual to locate the adjusters on your fence.

To make the adjustment, slip a pair of 1½- to 2-inch-wide wood blocks into one of the miter slots. The blocks should fit without extra play. Place one near the front of the saw and the other at the back. Slide the rip fence until it touches one or both blocks. You'll know the fence is parallel to the miter slot if it touches both blocks simultaneously. If it touches just one block, loosen the adjustment bolts or back out the adjustment screws and shift the fence body until it also touches the second block. Tighten the adjustment bolts or snug up the screws to hold the fence in this new position. Check the action of the fence by clamping it to the front rail. The fence body should remain parallel to the miter slot. If it doesn't, readjust the bolts or screws and try clamping it down again. Some low-quality fences simply won't stay aligned. If your saw has one of these, consider replacing it with a better aftermarket fence. Otherwise, the fence will never yield accurate cuts.

In addition to being parallel to the miter slots, the rip fence must also be square to the saw table. Check yours by standing a square on the saw table and against the fence face. If the fence tips into or away from the square, you may be able to adjust this condition by turning setscrews on the fence clamp. Otherwise, you can square up a fence by attaching a piece of plywood or hardwood to the

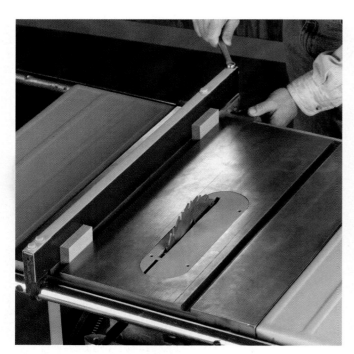

Check the alignment of the rip fence by placing it against blocks of wood in the miter slot. The rip fence should touch both blocks evenly. If it doesn't, adjust the fence until it does.

Use a square to see whether the rip fence face meets the saw table at 90°. Using the fence setscrews, tune the fence until it meets the table squarely. For a fence without setscrews, insert shims behind the faces.

fence to act as an auxiliary fence, then insert a few paper or soda-can shims behind the auxiliary fence to bring the fence faces into square.

Adjusting the blade tilt controls. All table saws have adjustable stops for setting the blade to 90° and 45°. Generally, these amount to a pair of stop bolts with lock nuts that make contact with the saw table or trunnions when the blade is tilted fully or set to 90°. To adjust the stops, you'll need to first locate the appropriate bolts inside your saw. The owner's manual will identify where these adjustment bolts are. Some saws, particularly newer cabinet saws, may have the 90° and 45° tilt stops located on top of the saw table to make adjustment much easier. They'll probably be a pair of recessed Allen screws near the throat plate. With this system, there's no need to grope for stop bolts inside the saw base.

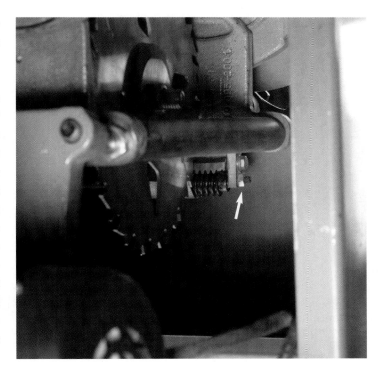

To make the adjustments, loosen the locknuts on the stop bolts or back out the Allen screws a few turns to provide extra range of blade motion. Crank the blade so the tilt stop pointer reads 0°, and check the blade angle with a try square. Crank the handwheel to bring the blade body flat against the square, then snug up the 90° stop bolt or Allen screw. Tighten the lock nut, if there is one. Follow the same procedure for adjusting the 45° stop. Tilt the blade until the bevel gauge reads 45°, and check the blade with a 45° drafting triangle. Snug up the stop bolt or Allen screw when the blade rests flat against the triangle. Finally, loosen the screw that holds the tilt stop pointer in position, and adjust the pointer so it reads 45° or 90° again. (It probably shifted position when you adjusted the stop bolts or screws.)

On most saws, the blade tilt stops are found inside the sawbase. Usually they are setscrews or bolts that you adjust with the blade set to 45° or 90°.

As a general rule of thumb, don't place much faith in the accuracy of these tilt stops. Cranking the blade from one extreme to the other will occasionally bang the stop bolts or screws out of position. Accumulated sawdust on the adjusters will affect the blade tilt settings. Even tilting the blade on a contractor's saw can torque the arbor assembly just enough to throw the blade a bit off the angle you want. The most reliable way to check your blade tilt setting is to keep a drafting triangle and try square handy and check your blade setting against these known angles. For establishing other blade angles, set a bevel gauge to the appropriate angle with a protractor, then tilt the blade so it rests against the bevel gauge.

Some saws have the blade tilt stop adjustments right on the saw table. Typically these are a pair of Allen bolts located near the throatplate. Loosen the stop bolts first, and use a square or drafting triangle to set the blade to the correct angle. Snug up the blade tilt stop bolts to lock the blade settings.

Adjusting the miter gauge. The miter gauge serves as a crosscutting feature on your saw. It's really just a protractor mounted on a bar with a fence formed along the flat edge. Miter gauges are basically all alike: to set an angle, swivel the protractor head until its pointer reaches the angle you need on the protractor scale, then tighten down the handle to lock the setting. Protractors often have a flipper stop and three setscrews to help set the gauge to 90° and 45°

Use a combination square as a reference to adjust the miter gauge stop screws.

quickly. These are what need adjustment from time to time.

To fine-tune the angle stops, back out the setscrews a few turns to provide some play at these stopping points, and loosen the push handle. Set the miter gauge on a flat surface, and hold a combination square so the square's perpendicular fence rests against the miter gauge bar and the rule touches the miter fence. Adjust the miter gauge head until the fence and rule are entirely flush, then tighten down the miter handle to lock it. Tip the flipper stop up, and gently turn the 90° stop screw in until it touches but doesn't deflect the flipper stop. Depending on the quality of your miter gauge, the flipper may have a bit of side-to-side play. This will limit the accuracy of the flipper. Adjust the 45° setscrew the same way. Use the 45° fence on the combination square this time as a reference for this gauge angle. Once the stops are adjusted, move the protractor's pointer as needed until it lines up with the 90° or 45° reference lines on the protractor scale.

If your miter gauge bar fits loosely in the miter slots, tighten the fit by raising a series of dimples along the edges of the bar with a center punch and ball-peen hammer. Set the bar against a workbench to tap these dimples about every inch or so along both edges of the bar. Try the fit again on the saw. If the bar slides sluggishly now, file the edges of the dimples slightly with a fine metal file to relax the fit. NOTE: Better quality miter gauges now come with tiny Allen screws threaded into the edges of the bar for adjusting excessive bar play. Turn these screws out slightly to improve the fit.

Raise dimples along the miter gauge bar to create a more snug fit in the miter slots.

Tuning the splitter & antikickback pawls. There aren't many improvements you can make to the standard-issue guard assembly that comes with your saw. It's important, however, that the splitter lines up behind the blade to keep workpieces from catching it and hanging up during a cut. This tendency to come out of alignment is partly why many woodworkers remove the guard and splitter altogether.

To align the splitter, check your owner's manual for the fasteners that hold the splitter in position. There may be a single nut threaded onto a shaft that holds the splitter, or the splitter may wrap around and into the back of the saw and mount with a few bolts to the rear trunnion. Whatever the arrangement, loosen the mounting fasteners slightly so the splitter will move but isn't floppy.

AFTERMARKET SPLITTERS

If the splitter and antikick-back pawls on your saw are difficult to adjust or remove, you may be able to replace them with an aftermarket splitter and pawls. These helpful accessories are sold through woodworking tool supply houses and fit a number of popular contractor's and cabinet saw brands. Most have a quick-release feature that allows you to remove the splitter by pulling a spring-loaded pin or pushing a button. You'll appreciate this convenience in dadoing situations where the workpiece isn't being split in two and the splitter must be removed. The accessory splitter doesn't come with an integral guard, however. The guard must be added separately.

Align the standard splitter that comes with your saw by sandwiching it and the blade between a pair of wood scraps. The splitter should be thinner than the blade and not touch either scrap when it is properly aligned.

Raise the blade to full height, and sandwich the blade and splitter between a pair of straightedges. Be sure the straightedges touch the blade body and not the carbide teeth. Pivot the splitter until it's spaced evenly between the straight-edges without touching either one. As best you can, hold the splitter in this position while tightening the mounting fasteners.

Also check the antikickback pawls. They're the spring-loaded plates with pointed teeth mounted on the splitter. The pawls are designed to keep workpieces moving in one direction through the blade—from infeed to outfeed. In the event of kickback, the pawl teeth should bite into the wood and stop it from propelling back toward you. This only happens if the teeth are sharp and there's enough spring pressure to hold the pawls firmly against the wood.

Sharpen the antikickback pawls with a file so they will catch the workpieces.

Check the action of the pawls by making a rip cut down the center of a piece of ¾-inch-thick scrap lumber about 3 feet long and 6 or 8 inches wide. Stop the cut once you've fed 1 foot through the blade, and shut off the saw. Try to pull the wood back out of the cut. If the pawls don't catch the workpiece, remove them from the splitter and sharpen the tips of the teeth with a file. Try the test again. If the teeth still fail to catch the wood, you may need to lower the entire splitter to create more spring pressure against the wood. Elongate the splitter mounting holes with a file, if possible, to drop the splitter and shift the pawls closer to the saw table.

NOTE

The blade guard and splitter have been removed for clarity in the photos in this chapter. A blade guard and splitter should always be used when making rip cuts.

Chapter 4
RIPPING

Ripping, or making a rip cut, cuts a board into two strips along the grain. Rip cuts typically divide a board lengthwise into parts with parallel, flat edges. Virtually every piece of lumber in your shop will need to be ripped at some point for further processing, and likely as not, you'll turn to the table saw to tackle these cuts. With its adjustable rip fence and large, stable work surface, a table saw makes ripping precise, easy, and fast. No other machine or hand tool performs rip cuts as well.

The basic procedure for ripping can be used to size stock of ordinary widths and lengths. We'll cover the general ripping method first. Be sure to read further in the chapter about how to manage other rip cuts on less typical stock. Long, thick, thin, short, or narrow workpieces may need to be ripped with special care or using accessories to make the technique safer. Kickback is common during ripping because the blade remains in the wood longer than during other cutting operations. Read the box on page 80 to learn more about kickback and how to avoid it.

Basic ripping techniques

Preliminary surfacing. To make rip cuts accurately and safely, start with stock that has at least one flat edge and one flat face to align against the rip fence and saw table. It's never safe to rip a board with an edge that rests unevenly against the rip fence or with a face that tips or rocks when you push it through the blade. So, the first step in ripping most lumber actually begins at the jointer and planer to create a flat edge and face.

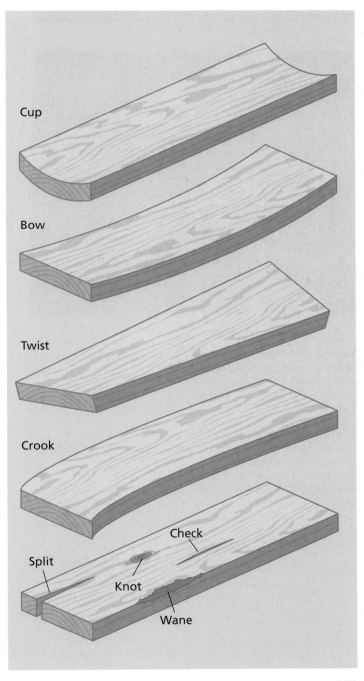

Cup

Bow

Twist

Crook

Check

Split

Knot

Wane

There are a variety of naturally occurring defects in lumber, and the top four in this illustration must be corrected before you can safely rip a board on a table saw. The tools for flattening cupped, bowed, twisted, and crooked boards are the jointer and planer. You'll need to create one flat edge and face with these machines. Other defects, such as waney edges or splits, won't affect rip cuts provided the board edge is flat.

Flatten the edge of the work-piece by making repeated passes over the jointer, then do the same with the board's face (top).

Flatten the opposite face of the workpiece using a surface planer. Then alternate from one face to the other to plane the board to final thickness (above).

Not all lumber needs to be jointed or planed before you can perform rip cuts, especially if you buy boards already surfaced smooth on the faces and edges. To determine whether you need to joint or plane a board to create the reference surfaces, hold it on edge and sight along the length. If the edge rises or dips, it isn't flat enough for ripping. Likewise, if the board is twisted or cupped across its face, you'll need to flatten it on a jointer and planer or crosscut it into shorter, flatter workpieces. Do not cut excessively warped boards on the table saw. In fact, you're probably better off turning severely warped lumber into fireplace kindling. More than likely it contains internal stresses that will make it warp again even after it's cut into smaller project parts.

Flatten the reference edge of a board by passing it several times over a jointer set for a light cut—1/32 inch is a good depth setting. You'll know the edge is flat when the jointer shaves the entire length of the board each time you make a pass. Check for edge flatness with a long straightedge or by sliding it over your saw table on edge and looking for gaps. Once you have a flat reference edge, flatten one board face on the jointer. Then run the board through a surface planer with the flat face down to smooth the other face and bring the board to the desired thickness. It's best to plane both faces of lumber, even though you only need one flat face for ripping. Alternate the board faces with each pass to remove an equal amount of material. This keeps the moisture content of the board about the same on each face so it will be less likely to warp again.

Preparing a saw for ripping. Every time you make a rip cut, you'll need to spend a few minutes setting up the saw. Over time, this prep work becomes second nature. If you're just beginning to use a table saw, here's what to do before making a rip cut:

Choose a blade. See pages 28 to 33 for more information on selecting a suitable blade for ripping. Whether you use a dedicated ripping blade or an all-purpose or combination blade, be sure the blade is sharp and the arbor nut is tightened securely against the spindle washer. If your saw is rated for 1½ hp or less, consider using a thin kerf blade for ripping.

Setting blade height. One of those endless debates among woodworkers is how high to set the saw blade for cutting. You have three height options here: Setting the blade low, so just the top ¼ inch of the blade teeth rise above the board; setting the blade high to expose most or all of the blades cutting range; or raising the blade to medium height so just the blade teeth and gullets rise above the workpiece. From the standpoint of safety, setting the blade low offers you the best protection from the teeth, but it creates a gradual blade arc that keeps many teeth in the wood during cutting. More teeth inside the workpiece leads to scorching and swirl marks. It also increases your risk of kickback. In contrast, cranking the blade all the way up forms a steep blade arc and leaves the fewest teeth in the saw kerf during ripping. You'll get much smoother, cleaner cuts with the blade dialed high, but you put your hands at greater risk with so much of the blade exposed. The best option is usually a medium height setting. Raise the blade so the bottom of the gullet just clears the top of your workpiece. At this height, the blade can clear the chips efficiently so the saw won't bog down in the cut, and the cut edges will be reasonably smooth with fewer burn marks or swirls.

Regardless of which blade height setting you choose, be sure the blade is set square to the saw table if you intend to cut square edges. Crank the blade up to full height and check it for squareness with a try square or combination square. Then lower the blade to your preferred cutting height.

Setting the cutting width. Most right-handed woodworkers tend to make rip cuts with the fence positioned to the right of the saw blade. Left-handers generally slide the fence over to the left side of the blade instead. As long as the blade is square to the table, it doesn't matter which side of the blade the fence is on. Choose the side that's most comfortable for you and offers the greatest workpiece support. If you need to tilt the blade for making an angled rip cut, you're actually cutting a bevel. Depending on which direction your blade tilts, you'll need to position the fence to the left or right of the blade. Read more about setting up bevel cuts on page 78.

Typically, the area you leave between the rip fence and the blade forms the width of your workpiece, and the material you cut free on the other side of the blade is the waste piece. This is just a general guideline. In some instances, you may want to set up the cut so the piece formed outside the blade and rip fence is the actual part you want to make. Whichever way you set up the cut, it's

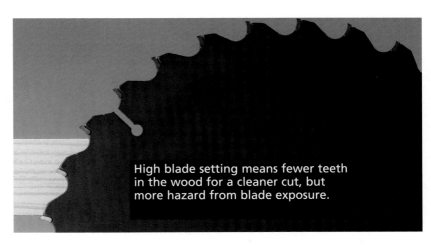

High blade setting means fewer teeth in the wood for a cleaner cut, but more hazard from blade exposure.

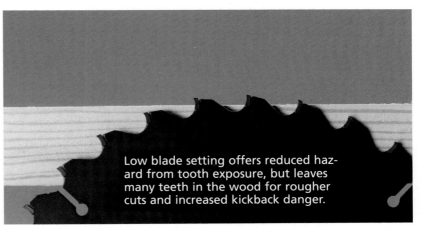

Low blade setting offers reduced hazard from tooth exposure, but leaves many teeth in the wood for rougher cuts and increased kickback danger.

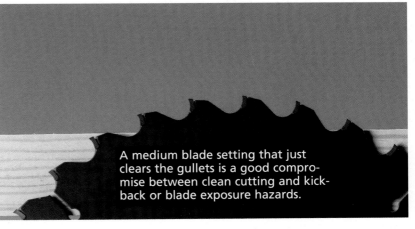

A medium blade setting that just clears the gullets is a good compromise between clean cutting and kickback or blade exposure hazards.

The three blade height options are setting the blade at maximum height to expose the blade's full cutting range (top), setting the blade low so only the top ¼ inch of teeth are visible above the board (middle), and setting the blade at medium height so just the teeth and gullets are visible above the board (above). Notice the relative number of teeth that are inside the wood during the cut. Fewer teeth are better for cleaner cuts.

Use a combination square to make sure your blade is square to the saw table (below).

Measure the distance between the rip fence and blade to set up a cutting width (middle).

The workpiece can be formed either between the blade and the rip fence, or on the outside of the blade away from the rip fence (bottom).

important to keep the blade kerf in mind when indexing the rip fence and blade. About ⅛ inch of material will be lost to the blade kerf, whether your workpiece is made between the fence and blade or outside this tunnel.

To set the width of cut, use a metal rule, tape measure, or the index scale on the front fence rail to determine the distance between the blade and rip fence. If you intend to create a workpiece of a specific width between the fence and blade, measure from the fence to the inside surface of the blade teeth to determine the exact width of cut. The common mistake in this scenario is to measure to the outer edge of the blade rather than the inner edge. Make this error, and you'll end up with a workpiece that's exactly one kerf width narrower than the width you want. It's a good habit to verify your fence setting at least twice when the fence is locked in place and before making the cut. You'll keep more workpieces out of the scrap bin this way. Be sure the fence is securely locked in place on its rails.

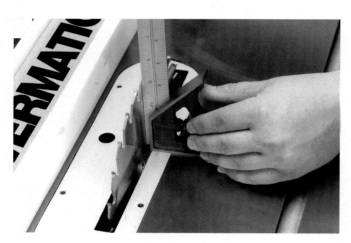

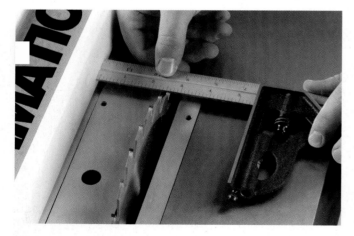

Featherboards & push sticks. In addition to having a blade guard and splitter in place for ripping, featherboards and push sticks are other important safety devices to have at the ready. Featherboards help keep workpieces pressed firmly against the saw table and rip fence as they enter the blade. They're especially beneficial when ripping long workpieces and standing back from the saw. In these cases, it is more difficult to keep workpieces tight against the saw table and rip fence as you walk them into the blade.

Clamp one featherboard to the saw table on the infeed side of the blade with the "feathers" facing the rip fence. Clamp a second featherboard to the rip fence so it lines up with the one mounted to the saw table. Position both featherboards just far enough from the blade so they won't interfere with the blade guard. Adjust both featherboards so they press against the workpiece and hold it firmly but not so tightly that they restrict your ability to push the board forward. This amount of tension should stop the workpiece from sliding backward and out of the blade when you pull on it. Test the action of the featherboards by sliding the board between them with the blade lowered below the saw table. If you'll be making multiple rip cuts on stock of different widths, reposition the featherboards each time the stock width changes.

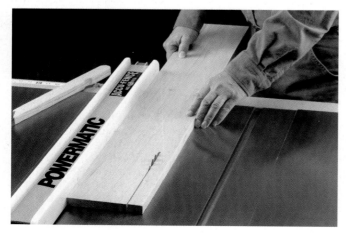

Have at least one push stick within easy reach during ripping. Two push sticks is even better, so you'll have one for each hand. A push stick is essential when ripping stock narrower than 1 foot. A tunnel this narrow affords too little room for pushing the wood safely past the blade by hand. If the waste piece that will be cut free on the outside of the blade will be narrower than 6 inches, have a second push stick ready for your other hand to sweep this piece clear of the blade. Once you develop the habit of using push sticks for ripping, the procedure won't feel safe without them. Lay your push sticks on the saw table so they are well clear of the blade and the workpiece. (See page 48 for more information on push stick styles.)

Final preparations. For boards longer than 4 feet, set up an outfeed support device such as a roller stand behind the saw to keep workpieces and waste material from tipping as they leave the saw table. When ripping boards longer than 8 feet, you may even want to position an additional roller stand in front of the saw to help support the board's weight as you feed it into the blade. Set these devices about half the board's length away from the saw. Use a shorter piece of lumber or a straightedge extended from the saw to set the height of the outfeed support device. Boards usually begin to sag as they leave the saw, so you'll want to set the bearing surface of the roller stand slightly lower than the saw table height. Otherwise, the sawn wood may hang up on the support and even push it out of the way or tip it over. Check the height by sliding the actual workpiece over the saw table and onto the outfeed support before ripping.

While you are making this check, be sure there's plenty of clear space on both the infeed and outfeed sides of the saw to complete the rip cut. If you are using

Set up a roller stand in front of the saw to support long boards that need to be ripped. Or start a few steps back from the front of the saw and slowly walk the board through the cut.

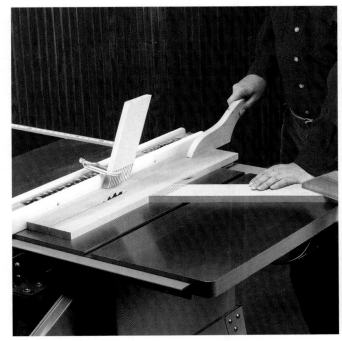

Featherboards clamped to the rip fence and saw table hold workpieces securely during a rip cut. Be sure to install them just in front of the blade—not behind it.

Place a straightedge on the saw table and set the outfeed roller ¼ inch lower than the table top.

Start a rip cut by standing to the left of the workpiece, placing your left leg against the corner of the saw with your hip touching the front fence rail.

Feed the workpiece into the blade with your right hand while pressing the board against the fence with your left hand.

a work table as a support device, clear it off before ripping. Reroute any extension cords and clear the floor to avoid tripping. Be sure the saw is resting squarely on the floor. If your saw is mounted on a rolling base, lock the casters to keep the machine from accidentally moving. For benchtop saws, clamp the saw base to a sturdy stand or worksurface. Check the splitter alignment behind the blade before making rip cuts to ensure the blade won't hang up on the splitter (see page 64).

Put on your protective safety gear, especially eye and ear protection, and roll up loose-fitting long sleeves to keep them from catching in the blade. As a final measure of security, you can rehearse your cutting technique with the actual workpiece before turning on the saw. Be sure you are comfortable with the process and your set-up.

Standard ripping procedure. For boards between 4 to 8 feet in length, here's the process for ripping: Start the saw and set the board on the saw table a few inches in front of the blade. Be sure the flat reference edge is against the rip fence and a flat board face is down on the saw table. Stand to the left of the workpiece if the fence is positioned on the right side of the blade. Wrap your right hand around the end of the board and press the board against the fence with your left hand along the left board edge. (Switch your body position to the right of the workpiece if the fence is left of the blade.)

For boards less than 4 feet long, you'll be able to stand close enough to the saw to place your left foot against the left corner of the saw base. If you can rest your left hip against the fence rail, do that as well to help maintain your center of balance. Longer boards force you to stand away from the saw, but position your left foot and hip against the saw as soon as you are close enough to do so. The closer you can keep your body to the saw, the better you'll be able to feed work past the blade without bending or reaching. Never reach over a spinning saw blade for any reason.

As you near the end of the cut, use a push stick to feed the board past the blade.

When the board severs in two, a wastepiece will be left next to the blade. Don't reach for it by hand.

Slide the board forward until it engages the blade teeth, then feed the wood into the blade with steady, even pressure. Use your right hand to push the wood and your left hand to hold it against the fence. Let the board edge slide against the fingers of your left hand rather than gripping the wood. If you must advance long boards by walking them into the saw, move forward in controlled steps. You'll know you are doing this if the motor keeps up with your progress. If the motor starts to labor, slow down your feed rate so the blade can build up speed again. For the cleanest cuts, feed the wood into the blade as rapidly as the motor will allow. Cutting too slowly or pausing mid-cut will leave blade marks.

With the workpiece clear of the blade, use the push stick to slide the wastepiece away from the blade.

While feeding the board into the saw, keep your eye on the joint where the board edge meets the rip fence. There should be no gap here during cutting. If the wood begins to veer away from the fence, apply more lateral pressure against the board with your left hand. You may also have to gently shift the board one way or the other with your right hand to correct the problem, but make this adjustment gradually. The primary purpose of your right hand is to push, not to steer.

When the back end of the board approaches the front of the saw table, slide your left hand back to a stationary position on the saw table at least 6 inches in front of the blade. Continue to use your left hand as a featherboard, but do not move it closer to the blade. Once the board end reaches the front edge of the saw table, hold it steady with your left hand and reach for the right push stick with your right hand. Fit the push stick notch over the end of the board and continue to advance the board past the blade until the end is clear.

WHAT TO DO IN THE EVENT OF A STALL

Sometimes during a rip cut, the board's kerf will spread open or close up behind the blade. When the kerf closes, it pinches the splitter, making it harder to advance the cut. If the kerf spreads open, the portion of the workpiece between the fence and blade can press against these surfaces creating friction. In either scenario, if you are using an underpowered saw or a dull blade, the blade may slow to the point of stalling. When the blade stops spinning while the motor is still on, you are dangerously close to experiencing a kickback. Shut off the saw immediately with your left hand and keep a firm grip on the wood with your right. Never let go of a workpiece when the saw is still powered up or it will expel the wood with great force. If you are standing away from the front of the saw for making a rip cut on long stock and the saw begins to stall, slow down your feed rate. You may even need to momentarily stop feeding the board to keep from overwhelming the saw motor and stopping the blade. When you can't reach the "Off" button, try to keep the blade spinning until you can safely turn off the machine or complete the cut.

When the waste piece to the left of the blade is cut free, you can either slide it away from the blade laterally with a push stick or leave it where it is and shut down the saw. Do not remove the waste by hand or retrieve your workpiece until the blade stops spinning.

Ripping long stock. We've already reviewed the process of handling a board when standing away from the front of the saw. Another technique for beginning the cut is to lift the back end of the board higher than the saw table. Doing this will press the front board edge firmly down on the table. Once the cut is under way, gently lower the back of the board so it's even with the saw table. You won't need to raise the board this way if you attach a featherboard to the rip fence to hold the board down during ripping.

If you don't have a spare roller stand to set in front of the saw for supporting long boards, elevate the back end of the board several inches above the front end. Doing this keeps the front end down on the saw table.

A roller stand positioned in front of the saw can help support the weight of a long board when beginning the cut. If you don't have one available, ask a helper to give you a hand. Have this person support the back end of the board and stand behind you while you feed the board into the blade. The role of the helper is to simply hold the board up, not to feed it or steer it along. When the back end of the board advances close enough for you to reach, grab the end with your right hand and have the helper step aside. Complete the rip on your own as usual.

When ripping short boards, use a push stick to make the entire cut. Don't hold short workpieces by hand.

A helper can also serve as outfeed support when necessary. Have your helper stand in back of the saw and receive the lumber as it leaves the saw table. Again, a helper's job is to support the board weight, but not to pull or steer the work behind the saw, which could bind the wood against the blade. Have the helper cup his or her hands beneath the wood and back up slowly as the wood moves forward.

Ripping short stock. The safest way to manage a rip cut on a workpiece shorter than 10 inches is to rip it from a longer piece of stock first, then crosscut the length you need. Sometimes you'll have no choice but to start from a short piece of stock. If the stock is wide enough to provide at least 6 inches of clearance between the fence and blade, make the rip as usual with a push stick. Slide the workpiece past the blade with a push stick in your right hand. Use diagonal pressure against the rip fence as you advance the push stick to keep the workpiece from skewing into the blade.

For stock that's narrow as well as short, you may be tempted to remove the guard to make more room around the blade for a push stick. Don't do it. Instead, set the workpiece in a crosscut sled or on a sliding miter table and make the rip as you would a crosscut without using the rip fence (see page 92).

Ripping narrow stock. Ripping long, narrow strips for glass retainers or trim requires a different procedure than for narrow rips on short stock. Start with stock that's at least 18 inches long and more than 6 inches wide. If you only need to rip one narrow strip, set up the cut so the "waste" on the outside of the blade actually becomes the workpiece you want to make. The stock between the rip fence and blade is merely extra material. When the narrow strip requires a profile of some sort along the edge, rout the profile first on the wide stock, then rip this profiled edge free to make the workpiece you need.

In cases where you want to cut multiple narrow strips, you have two options. If the workpieces are wide enough to allow you to guide them with a narrow push stick, set the rip fence so the tunnel between the fence and blade matches the width of the strips you need. Rip the strips one after the next using the narrow push stick.

A second method is useful if the strips are too narrow to be guided between the fence and blade with a push stick. In these cases, build a pushing jig from stock that's at least 6 inches wide. Attach a strip of wood along the back end with a lip that extends past one edge of the board. Have the length of the lip match the

For ripping particularly short and narrow workpieces, use a sliding miter table or crosscut sled instead of the rip fence. Make the short rip like you would a crosscut.

To rip matching narrow strips, set up the cut so the strips are formed between the rip fence and blade rather than on the outboard side of the blade.

A "notched" pushing jig placed between the rip fence and workpiece also allows you to rip narrow strips—this time on the outboard side.

width of the strips you need to make. Fasten a handle to the pushing jig to keep your hand up and clear of the blade.

To rip the strips, set a piece of stock against the jig so it rests on the lip. Move the stock and the jig past the blade together to rip the first strip. Repeat the process to make more strips. Be sure to use a zero-clearance throat plate when ripping very narrow strips to keep the strips from falling down into the blade slot as they're cut free (see page 59).

Ripping thin stock. Cutting thin stock such as plastic laminate is possible to do on the table saw, provided there's no gap between the rip fence and the saw table when the fence is clamped down tight. If there's a gap greater than ⅟₁₆ inch, thin materials can slip under the fence during cutting and ruin the cut or lead to a kickback. You can avoid these problems by attaching an auxiliary fence to the rip fence to cover the gap. It's a good idea to install an auxiliary fence if your rip fence only clamps to the front fence rail—the outfeed end of the fence is prone to lifting slightly when it's only clamped down in front. You could also pull the outfeed end of the fence down tight to the saw table with a clamp if that eliminates the gap.

The auxiliary fence can be made from any scrap wood or sheet material with a flat face and edge. Attach the fence to your rip fence with screws, bolts, or a clamp. Press it firmly against the saw table before tightening the fasteners.

If you are cutting plastic laminate, hold the laminate down against the table with a long-soled push stick to keep it from fluttering and possibly chipping during cutting. For chip-free edges, make the cuts using a triple-chip tooth laminate cutting blade with a negative hook angle, or use a sharp ATB blade.

If you need to rip thin materials such as laminate, attach an auxiliary fence to your rip fence to eliminate any gap that may exist between the fence and saw table.

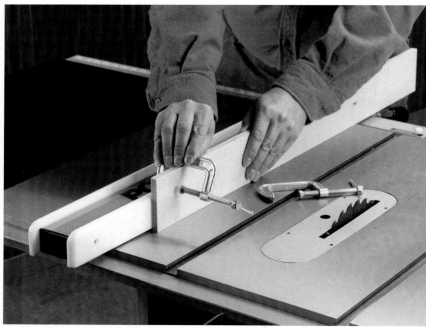

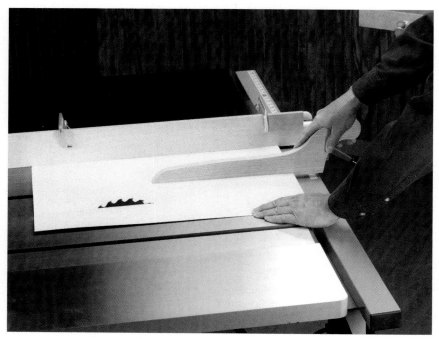

Guide laminate through the blade, pressing the material against the auxiliary rip fence like a normal rip cut on wood. Use a long-soled push stick to help keep the laminate from lifting off the saw table as you make the cut.

Ripping thick stock. Occasionally you may need to rip a plank or post that's thicker than the maximum cutting height of your saw blade. Any workpiece thicker than about 3⅛ inches will exceed the cutting depth of most benchtop and contractor's saws.

The safest machine to use in these instances is a band saw. Band saws have thin blades that can slice through thick material without overheating. Even a small band saw has a greater depth of cut than a table saw. The linear path of the blade also eliminates kickback problems associated with tools that have circular blades.

The trouble with cutting thick stock on a table saw with a conventional guard and splitter is that the wood will interfere with the mounting posts on the splitter that hold the antikickback fingers. The only way to carry out the cut is to remove the splitter and guard, which is never a safe practice. One solution is to outfit your saw with an overarm blade guard (see page 83). This guard style doesn't include a splitter, and most don't have antikickback devices, but the guard at least shields your hands from the blade. Without at least a guard in place, ripping thick stock isn't safe on a table saw.

If you have an overarm guard installed on your saw, here's how to rip a thick workpiece: Set the blade for maximum height and adjust it so it's 90° to the saw table. Flatten all four edges and faces of the workpiece using a jointer and planer so the stock will rest flat against the rip fence and table. Pass the stock through the saw blade, adjusting your feed rate as needed to keep the blade from stalling as it makes the deep cut. Use extreme caution here, especially if there's no splitter to keep the saw kerf from closing up behind the blade. After making the first pass, flip the workpiece over and make a second cut with the same reference edge against the fence. If the second pass doesn't split the workpiece, you'll need to complete the kerf with a hand saw.

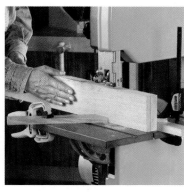

The safest way to rip very thick stock is to use a band saw rather than a table saw. The linear path of the band saw blade eliminates the kickback hazard.

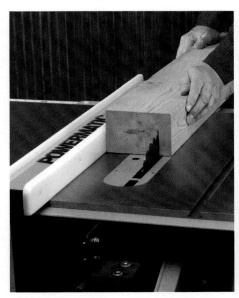

When ripping thick stock that exceeds the blade capacity, make the first pass with the blade set at maximum blade height.

Flip the workpiece over and make a second pass to complete the kerf. If the blade still doesn't reach, you'll have to finish the cut with a hand saw.

Resawing is another operation that falls into the category of ripping thick stock. Resawing is typically a process of slicing thin sheets from the face of a board to create veneer. The technique requires standing the board on edge. The correct resawing machine is a bandsaw, not a table saw. It will be difficult to keep a wide board from tipping away from the rip fence on a table saw unless the board is at least 2 inches thick. If you don't own a band saw, buy your veneer instead of attempting to make it on a table saw.

Bevel-ripping. Any time you tilt the blade to an angle and make a rip cut, you're technically cutting a bevel, or bevel-ripping. Beveled edges are commonly used around the center panels of cabinet doors or as a means of easing sharp edges. When the bevel only nibbles a portion of the edge away, the treatment is called a chamfer. Chamfers help protect the edges and corners of furniture or cabinetry while also serving as decorative details.

The process for cutting bevels is largely the same as making standard rip cuts, but there are a few special considerations to keep in mind. For one, position the rip fence on the side of the blade opposite the direction it tilts. If your blade tilts right, the rip fence belongs on the left side of the table. This way, the waste piece that's cut free during bevel-ripping doesn't become trapped between the fence and table where the blade can catch it and throw it back your way. The waste also ends up resting on the table below the blade rather than on top where the teeth can catch and throw it.

One problem with conventional, right-tilting saws is that the table area to the left of the blade is sometimes smaller than the area on the right. Left-tilting saws solve this table shortage problem for bevel-ripping. The blade tilts left, which leaves plenty of workspace on the right for setting the fence and situating the workpiece.

Align the workpiece cutting line with the blade, and slide the rip fence against the workpiece. Be sure to do this set-up with the saw unplugged, for safety.

When making beveled rip cuts, tilt the blade away from the rip fence so the waste piece ends up below the blade.

To make a bevel with the workpiece laying flat on the saw table, tilt the blade and clamp the fence in place. It helps to draw an angled reference line on your workpiece to help line up the blade before you make the cut. Or, start the saw and slide the workpiece forward until the blade teeth just "kiss" the workpiece at your reference mark. Turn off the saw and adjust the fence as needed to correct any misalignment. Feed the workpiece through the blade with your left hand if the fence is on the left or your right hand if the fence is positioned right of the blade. Use your other hand like a featherboard to hold the workpiece tight against the fence as you slide the wood along.

If you need to cut a bevel that's steeper than 45°, you'll have to stand the workpiece on edge instead of on its face. For boards wider than 8 inches, attach a tall auxiliary fence to the rip fence to help support the workpiece and keep it from teetering. Install a zero-clearance throat plate as well. The narrow blade slit on a zero-clearance throat plate prevents the board from tipping down into the blade opening. When the bevel you're cutting removes most or all of the board's supportive lower edge, clamp a piece of scrap to the board so it rides along the top of the auxiliary fence. The scrap will act like a runner and help keep the workpiece from tipping down into the blade slot.

Bevel-ripping tends to generate more blade marks and swirls than standard ripping. To help minimize these problems, check the alignment of the blade and rip fence. Tune the saw if you discover any blade heel (see page 61).

Ripping waney or crooked stock. Occasionally you'll find boards in the lumberyard rack with rough or bark-covered edges. As boards are sawn from a log, those closest to the perimeter of the trunk may not get ripped square prior to shipment and sale. When board edges are not square because of a natural defect, the condition is called wane.

For cutting steep bevels along the edge of a board, you may need to stand it up on the saw table. Make the cut with the workpiece against a tall auxiliary fence attached to the rip fence. Clamp a runner to the workpiece to ride on the auxiliary rip fence. This keeps the workpiece from drifting down into the throat plate blade slot.

If a board has two waney edges, make one edge flat by attaching a straight board and ripping one waney edge off. Once one edge of the workpiece is flat, remove the straight board and rip the workpiece as usual with the flat edge against the rip fence.

If only one edge is waney, rip off the defective edge with the board's flat edge against the rip fence, just as you would for any normal rip cut. You can also rip boards with two waney or crooked edges by creating a flat edge using a piece of flat-edged scrap. Fasten the scrap over one bad edge with small nails or screws. Trim off the waney or crooked edge by running the scrap and board through the saw with the flat-edged scrap riding against the rip fence. Then remove the scrap and flip the workpiece so the freshly sawn edge is against the fence. Trim off the second uneven edge.

KICKBACK & HOW TO AVOID IT

Table saw blades are designed to cut along the infeed teeth. Splitters prevent the blade teeth on the outfeed side of the blade from cutting the workpiece by holding the saw kerf open. If you don't use a splitter behind the blade, there's nothing to prevent the back teeth from either cutting the wood or grabbing it as they rise out of the saw table. When the latter condition happens, the blade can lift the workpiece off the saw and propel it in your direction at great force. This situation is called kickback, and it happens in a fraction of a second. When the blade grabs the wood, it can also place your hands in harm's way. There's no way your natural reflexes can save you during a kickback, but it's easy to avoid. Use a guard and splitter on your saw whenever you are making a cut that divides a workpiece in two. Keep your blades sharp and clean, and tune the saw to minimize blade heel. During cutting, always hold workpieces firmly against the saw table with either hand pressure, push sticks or by using featherboards. Don't stand directly behind the workpiece during cutting. If kickback does happen, at least you will be out of the way.

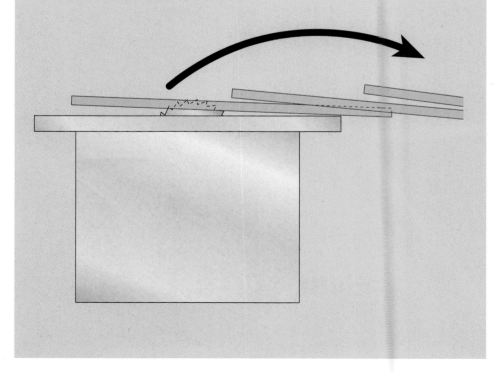

Using a partial fence

Some wood species with wavy or uneven grain may spread open behind the blade during a rip cut. This also happens with wet or distressed lumber. As the kerf widens, the wood between the fence and blade can twist or press against the splitter and make it more difficult to push past the blade. One way to create more clear space behind the blade is to attach a partial fence to your rip fence. A partial fence is just a piece of dimensionally stable scrap such as plywood or hardwood that mounts on the infeed side of the blade. It gets its name because the fence stops about an inch past the infeed blade edge, leaving the rest of the rip fence exposed. With this arrangement, workpieces can open up behind the blade as they're cut without binding against the blade, splitter, or fence. Make your partial fence adjustable by routing a through slot lengthwise so the fence can slide along the bolts or screws that attach it to the rip fence. Whenever you raise or lower the saw blade, loosen the mounting fasteners and slide the partial fence forward or backward to readjust it in relation to the infeed blade edge.

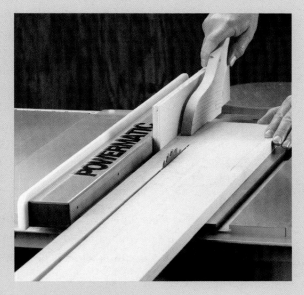

Ripping tapers. Tapers are rip cuts that follow the long grain but cut the edge of a board at an angle. You'll see tapers used most commonly on table and chair legs, and generally the legs are tapered on two adjacent edges. Tapers are an attractive way to slim down the proportions of furniture parts, and they're easy to cut on a table saw using a simple tapering jig. Do not attempt to cut tapers by holding a workpiece at an angle to the blade without anchoring it in a jig. There's no way to accurately make a freehand cut, and the wood will probably kick back in the process.

Tapering jigs sold in woodworking supply catalogs are relatively inexpensive and easy to use, or you can build your own. Fabricated tapering jigs are adjustable so you can use them for making a variety of tapers with different angles. They consist of two adjustable "arms" joined by a hinge on one end. One arm rides against the rip fence, and the other arm holds the workpiece at an angle to the blade. A stop on the end of this arm steadies the workpiece as you slide the jig and workpiece past the blade. An adjustable brace spanning both arms locks the arms in place.

One drawback to the two-arm-style tapering jig is that it doesn't have a feature that holds the workpiece tight

Tapered cuts are easy to make with an inexpensive tapering jig. The jig holds workpieces safely at an angle to the blade.

against the arm while you cut the taper. For tapers that don't run the length of a workpiece, you can secure a clamp to the workpiece and the adjustable arm outside the cutting area for added safety. On full-length taper cuts, there won't be room for a clamp. Use a push stick to steady the workpiece against the jig.

To cut tapers with an adjustable jig, begin by marking the workpiece with layout lines showing the tapered edge. Then use a straightedge and pencil to draw a line across the front of the saw table that shows the exact path of the saw blade. Set the straightedge against the side of the blade closest to the rip fence to mark this line. Place the tapering jig against the rip fence and the workpiece in the jig. Adjust the arm that holds the workpiece until the line you made on the workpiece aligns with the blade reference line on the table. Slide the rip fence closer to the blade if necessary, to help align the jig. Using the reference line on the saw table, you'll know exactly where the blade will enter the workpiece. Lock the jig arms and rip fence to hold their positions.

Back up the jig to the front of the table so the workpiece clears the blade. To cut the taper, slide the jig and workpiece along the fence as you would a normal rip cut. To cut a matching taper on an adjacent edge, flip the workpiece in the jig so the first taper faces up, then cut the second taper. To taper all four faces, reset the jig for twice the first angle when you have to place a tapered edge against the adjustable arm.

To set up a taper cut, draw a line on the saw table in front of the blade using a straightedge. This line shows the path of the saw blade.

Adjust the tapering jig to align your cut line with the path of the saw blade. Lock the jig at this setting. Slide the workpiece and jig past the blade to trim along the workpiece layout line.

Aftermarket guards

Guards and splitters that come with most table saws are a one-piece design. The metal or plastic shroud that covers the blade is attached to the splitter and pivots up and down to accommodate workpieces of varying thickness. A pair of antikickback pawls straddle the splitter on short posts.

While the design works reasonably well for ripping and crosscutting average-sized lumber, one-piece guard and splitter assemblies won't allow for cutting lumber thicker than the maximum blade height. For dadoing operations, the splitter must be removed, which means the guard goes, too. Even narrow rip cuts can be difficult with the guard in place, because there may not be enough room between the guard and the rip fence for maneuvering a push stick. Guards sometimes are difficult to see through or around for tracking the saw cut. Needless to say, there are many reasons why woodworkers remove the splitter and blade guard and never put them back on.

Fortunately, a number of aftermarket companies offer better blade guard options. These blade guard styles mount to the end of the extension wing or table, the ceiling above the saw, or even the floor. Instead of fastening to a splitter, the guard shroud attaches to an arm that may telescope, swivel, or crank up and down to provide for lateral and vertical adjustments. The shroud itself is generally made of thick acrylic plastic, and some shrouds have pivoting sides so the guard can partially ride up and over the rip fence when the fence must be placed close to the blade. When the guard assembly works independently of a splitter, you can keep it in place for non-through cuts, such as dadoes and rabbets. Some guards come with a separate splitter, but other styles do not.

Aftermarket blade guards are wonderful safety improvements, but they're expensive. You may pay nearly as much for the guard as you did for the whole saw. As of this writing, you'll only find aftermarket blade guards available for contractor's and cabinet saws. If you own a benchtop saw, you're stuck with the blade guard and splitter that come with it. If you own a saw that accepts an aftermarket guard, consider replacing it. Despite the initial cost, it's a great investment when compared to sawing without a guard or splitter and risking your fingers and hands.

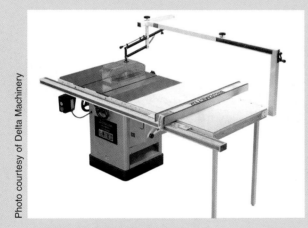

Photo courtesy of Delta Machinery

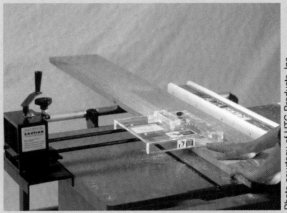

Photo courtesy of HTC Products, Inc.

Photo courtesy of Felder USA

NOTE

The blade guard and splitter have been removed for clarity in the photos in this chapter. A blade guard and splitter should always be used when making cross cuts.

Chapter 5
CROSSCUTTING

Crosscuts square the ends of a workpiece and cut it to length. As the name implies, crosscuts are made perpendicular to the grain direction rather than parallel to it, so they cross the grain. The distinction between rip and crosscuts becomes less important when it comes to cutting sheet materials such as plywood where there isn't a definite grain direction. (See pages 131 to 133 for more on cutting sheet materials.)

Table saws excel at rip cutting because the rip fence provides a long bearing surface to hold the work steady. Crosscuts aren't quite as foolproof or effective an operation on the table saw, but you can still cut them accurately. You'll use the miter gauge for making crosscuts instead of the rip fence. Since miter gauges have short fences, it's more difficult to hold workpieces securely and keep them aligned with the blade. The problem compounds when you need to swivel the miter gauge head for making mitered crosscuts. Later in this chapter you'll learn how to improve the performance of your miter gauge by adding an auxiliary fence or switching to a crosscut sled for performing some cuts. Either option will dramatically improve your cutting accuracy. In fact, you may even want to skip ahead to page 90 now and add an auxiliary fence before you begin making crosscuts. Once you've added an auxiliary fence to your miter gauge and realized its benefit, you'll probably never want to use a miter gauge without one.

Crosscuts may be a bit more challenging to make accurately, but they definitely have a leg up on rip cuts from a safety standpoint. To make a crosscut, hold the

Crosscuts are made with workpieces held against the miter gauge fence. Never use the rip fence for making crosscuts.

workpiece against the miter gauge, align the cutting line on the wood with the blade, then slide the miter gauge and workpiece past the blade to saw the board in two. Usually the waste piece is the portion left behind and next to the blade. Crosscutting doesn't involve the rip fence, so waste pieces aren't wedged into a tunnel between the rip fence and blade where they can kick back. Cross-grain cuts don't release internal stresses in lumber like long-grain rip cuts do, so the saw kerf stays open behind the blade.

Kickbacks are still possible when crosscutting. They'll probably happen if you make the mistake of sawing freehand instead of guiding workpieces with a miter gauge or crosscut sled. There's almost no way to make an accurate free-hand cut, and it's never safe to do so. If the wood twists even slightly during a crosscut, it will bind on the blade and get grabbed and thrown. Using the rip fence as a bearing surface for crosscuts can also invite kickback, especially if you are guiding a narrow end along the fence. As you slide the workpiece along the rip fence, it will almost inevitably pivot away from the fence and bind the blade. Similarly, never use the miter gauge in tandem with the rip fence to guide a workpiece along both an edge and an end. Rip fences should be reserved for ripping, crosscutting wide panels, and cutting sheet materials (see page 131) or as a clamping surface for a stop block to make repetitive crosscuts (see page 92).

Another cause for kickback during crosscutting is when waste pieces are short-er than the blade is wide or narrower than the blade opening in the throat plate. A good preemptive measure for controlling thin waste pieces is to install a zero-clearance throat plate on your saw. A tight blade slot keeps short, nar-row offcuts from dropping down into the blade slot and wedging against the blade where they can be thrown from the saw table. Be sure to saw with a guard and splitter in place to keep the blade from tossing short offcuts up and off the table.

ORDERING RIP AND CROSSCUTS

In most cases, a pair of rip cuts and crosscuts will bring workpieces to their final size with flat, square edges and ends. The order of these initial cuts depends on the condition of the lumber you are starting with. If the lumber is much longer than necessary, it's best to make a crosscut first to cut what you need to rough length. Then rip the board close to one edge and flatten this sawn edge on the jointer. Make a second rip along the opposite edge to size the workpiece to width. With both long edges parallel and flat, crosscut the ends to bring them into square with the edges as well as to trim the workpiece to length. If one edge of your lumber is already flat and smooth, you can rip the workpiece to width and crosscut to length in any order you like provided you use the flat edge as your reference against the miter gauge or rip fence for making the subsequent cuts.

Mark the waste side of a workpiece with an "X" so you can align the blade to cut on this side of the layout line. Once you're used to making crosscuts, cutting on the "waste" side becomes second nature.

Basic crosscutting techniques

Preparing for crosscutting. Before you make a basic square crosscut, there are a few preparations to make. First, use a combination square to check the setting of the miter gauge head in relation to the miter bar (see page 64). Loosen the handle and adjust the head so it's precisely perpendicular to the bar before proceeding. Next, raise the saw blade and use a square to verify that the blade is perpendicular to the saw table. If you are crosscutting a workpiece longer than 2 feet, install an auxiliary fence on your miter gauge to provide more workpiece support (see page 90). For lumber that will over-hang the saw table during crosscutting, set up a side support device next to the saw, such as a work table or a saw horse, with a bearing surface slightly below saw table height.

Mark your workpiece with a layout line across both the face of the board and the edge that will begin the cut. You'll need this edge layout line for aligning the workpiece with the blade. It never hurts to mark the portion that will be cut free as waste with an "X" so you'll be sure to cut on the waste side of the layout line. Otherwise you could end up with a workpiece that's a blade thickness too short. Be sure to slide the rip fence out of the way of the miter gauge and workpiece, and clear off any other debris that might interfere with the cut.

Basic crosscutting procedure. You can use either miter slot for guiding a crosscut when the blade is perpendicular to the saw table. If your saw has an accessory table that projects beyond the right extension wing, use this surface for supporting long workpieces with the miter gauge located in the right-hand miter slot. When the blade is tipped for bevel crosscuts, the miter slot you choose is dictated by how the blade tilts (see page 96). As a general

Align the blade carefully with the layout line before starting the saw and making the cut.

guideline, choose the miter slot that allows the gauge to support the longer section of the board, regardless of whether this portion will become the workpiece or the waste piece. Cut the shorter section free.

Hold or clamp the workpiece against the miter gauge fence and slide both up to the blade with the saw turned off. Set the blade to a height above the workpiece that's comfortable for you or to produce the cleanest cut (see page 69). Adjust the workpiece by sliding it along the miter fence until the layout line on the board edge is even with the blade teeth. Make sure the thickness of the blade falls on the waste side of your layout line.

With the workpiece and blade aligned, slide the miter gauge and workpiece away from the blade. Put on your safety glasses and ear protection, and roll up loose-fitting long sleeves to keep them clear. Check that the saw is resting squarely on the floor and cannot move, especially if it is on a rolling base. If you have any doubt about what you are going to do, rehearse your crosscutting technique with the actual workpiece before turning on the saw.

Start the saw. Position your body behind the miter gauge so you are standing clear of the blade path. If the miter gauge is to the right of the blade, hold the workpiece with your right hand and grip the miter gauge handle with your left

With the workpiece held firmly against the miter gauge, slide both past the blade to make the cut. Stand behind the miter gauge so your body is clear of the waste piece.

hand. Reverse the hand positions when the miter gauge is in the left miter slot. This way your arms aren't crossed over one another and both are clear of the blade.

Slide the miter gauge forward and gently feed the workpiece into the blade. As soon as the teeth engage the workpiece, move the gauge smoothly and rapidly past the blade so the teeth cut cleanly and without burning. When the workpiece cuts in two, a waste piece is left next to the blade. Continue to push the miter gauge forward and clear of the blade. Turn off the saw and remove the waste before proceeding with another crosscut. If the offcut is large, you may be able to sweep it away from the blade with a push stick without turning off the saw first, but it's always safer to turn off the saw.

Push the miter gauge past the blade until the workpiece is cut in two and the workpiece is clear.

Sometimes the piece you cut free is the workpiece you're actually making. In these cases, arrange your crosscuts so both ends of this workpiece will be square when you cut it to length. In other words, make one crosscut on the longer initial stock to square one end of your soon-to-be shorter workpiece, then crosscut the workpiece free and to length. Typically, it will take two crosscuts to make any final workpiece square on both ends. You'll make these cuts more safely by performing them on longer stock.

Slide the waste piece away from the blade with a push stick. If it is too small to reach easily, turn off the saw first. Do not remove short waste pieces by hand with the saw running.

ADDING A SHOP-MADE AUXILIARY MITER FENCE

Extending your miter gauge fence is an easy way to improve its supportive function during cross-cutting. All you need is a length of flat, square ¾-inch-thick hardwood scrap or stiff sheet material 12 to 24 inches long and 3 to 4 inches wide. If you're using the integrated guard and splitter that came with your saw, set the miter gauge in the slot next to the guard. Hold the auxiliary miter fence against the miter gauge so the end closest to the blade guard stops just short of making contact with it (below left). Attach the fence to the miter gauge with a couple short flathead machine screws driven through the holes in the miter gauge fence. Or you can use short carriage bolts and nuts, but countersink the bolt heads into the auxiliary wood fence. For miter gauge heads with no mounting holes, drill a pair of holes for this purpose. Another option is to buy a fence extension (below right) and attach it to your miter gauge. These devices usually are outfitted with an adjustable stop that slides along the length of the extension for setting up repetitive crosscuts. If you eventually upgrade to a precision aftermarket miter gauge, it will likely come with a fence extension.

 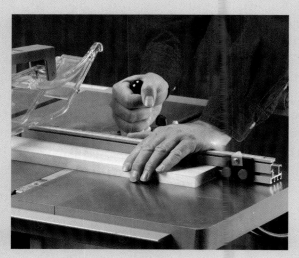

Crosscutting long workpieces. Crosscutting workpieces longer than 4 feet becomes increasingly difficult with a miter gauge, even one that's outfitted with an auxiliary fence. The closer you cut to the end of a long board, the more the board tends to pivot away from the miter fence toward the board's natural center of gravity when you push it through the blade. Even cuts made nearer to the board's center are difficult to make on long lumber simply because you are moving a heavy piece of wood over the saw table and trying to hold it tightly against the miter gauge at the same time.

Here are a couple of ways to crosscut long stock accurately and safely: In cases where lumber is more than 6 feet long and exceedingly heavy, choose a different tool to make the initial crosscuts. A circular saw guided against a straightedge, a power miter saw, or a hand saw are all safer choices for making these first crosscuts on long boards. In fact, power miter saws are becoming increasingly common in woodworking shops. They are wonderfully accurate machines for crosscutting board lumber, and you don't have to move the work past the blade to make the cut. With a power miter saw, you pivot the saw down or slide it through the wood, with the workpiece held stationary.

If you have no other tool options except a table saw for crosscutting long lumber, set the workpiece in a crosscut sled to make the cut. A crosscut sled provides more support than an auxiliary miter fence, and you'll have a broader surface to push the work evenly past the blade.

Without the aid of a crosscut sled, it's imperative to add an auxiliary fence to the miter gauge head. You may even want to make the auxiliary fence longer than 2 feet to improve its support or double it up to keep it from deflecting behind a heavy, long board. Attach a clamp to the auxiliary fence so it holds the workpiece down against the saw table when you make the cut. This way you can use your hand pressure to help push the work forward without also having to hold it down firmly to the table. Make the cut slowly and as smoothly as possible. It's a good idea to crosscut your workpieces slightly oversized to make the lengths more manageable, then cut them to final size. The second crosscuts will tend to be cleaner and more accurate than the first cuts from long boards. Be sure to set up a support surface beside the saw so long workpieces won't tip off the machine.

If a workpiece is too long to slide easily over the table saw, make the crosscut on a power miter saw or with a circular saw instead.

Crosscutting short pieces. The trouble with crosscutting small workpieces is that it's difficult to hold them down on the saw table and snug against the miter

Crosscutting long stock is easy with a crosscut sled and more accurate than using a miter gauge (left).

Use a side support device to keep long workpieces from tipping off the saw table during cutting. Here, we're using the edge of a scrap clamped to a sawhorse as the bearing surface (below).

Use a crosscut sled for crosscutting thin or short workpieces safely. Hold the workpiece firmly against the sled fence with a push stick.

fence with a pushstick, especially when you're also sliding the miter gauge forward. A better alternative is to crosscut short pieces in a crosscut sled where you can hold the work stationary with a push stick and slide the whole sled. If you don't have a crosscut sled, crosscut a short workpiece from a longer length of stock so you can keep your hand clear of the blade.

Repetitive crosscutting. Most woodworking projects will have some parts with matching lengths. You could measure and cut each of these like-sized parts individually, but the process is time-consuming, and odds are the part lengths won't be exactly the same in the end.

A better method for cutting several parts to precise, matching lengths is to use a stop block. A stop block is simply a piece of scrap with smooth, square edges and ends that you clamp temporarily to an auxiliary miter gauge fence, a crosscut sled, or the rip fence. Stop blocks create a fixed distance to the blade so you measure just once to cut as many same-length parts as you need.

When attaching a stop block to the auxiliary miter fence or the back fence of a crosscut sled, clamp the block on the same side of the blade as the workpiece you want to make. Position it so the distance between the block and the blade matches the workpiece length. Cut one end of the workpiece square, and butt this end against the stop block. If you need to make workpieces longer than the auxiliary fence, you may have to install a longer auxiliary fence.

Use a stop block clamped to the rip fence to set up repetitive crosscuts. Set the block well forward of the blade so the workpiece will clear it before it reaches the blade. Never make crosscuts with workpieces held against both the rip fence and the miter gauge. Otherwise, you'll trap the piece that is cut free, which could lead to a kickback.

Another option for making repetitive cross cuts is to clamp a stop block to an auxiliary fence on the miter gauge (left) or to the fence on a crosscut sled (above).

You can also use the rip fence as a mounting surface for a stop block, provided you follow a few safety requirements. First, be sure to clamp the stop block to the fence ahead of the blade on the infeed side. Place the stop block far enough forward of the blade so the full width of the workpiece clears the stop block before it engages the blade. It's a good idea to make the stop block from stock that's at least ¾-inch thick. With these provisions, the workpiece and the stop block are clear of one another so the workpiece can't jamb between the stop block and the blade, and cause a kickback. To index the cut, clamp the block to the fence, and mark your workpiece to length. Set the workpiece against the miter fence so the blade aligns with your cutting line. Slide the fence over until the stop block touches the end of the workpiece, and lock the fence. Make the cut by sliding the workpiece forward along the stop block, then off the block and into the blade.

Crosscutting miters. Crosscutting a standard miter involves pivoting the miter gauge head to an angle other than 0° and cutting the wood with the blade set square to the table. Miter gauges can be pivoted to cut angles up to 45°, which tends to be the most common angle for woodworking situations. Unless you are using a precision miter gauge with preset detents for locking exact angle settings, it's best not to trust the protractor markings on the miter gauge head. They're usually slightly inaccurate. Instead, set the head by using a drafting square or a bevel gauge locked to the cutting angle you need. To do this, place the triangle or bevel gauge against the saw blade body and position the miter gauge in a miter slot next to the blade. Pivot the miter head until it makes even contact with the reference tool, and lock the head setting. Cut a miter on test scrap to check the angle before cutting your actual workpiece.

To set precise miter angles, use a bevel gauge locked to the angle you need with the gauge held against both the saw blade and miter gauge. This yields a more accurate setting than using the protractor scale on the miter gauge.

Another handy way to set up a miter cut is to first mark the cutting line on both faces of your workpiece. Hold the workpiece flush against the miter gauge head and pivot it until the bar aligns with your cutting line. Lock the head here. Then flip the workpiece face down on the saw table. The gauge will cut your exact angle setting once you align the workpiece cutting line with the blade.

Miter cuts must be performed carefully or your wood joints won't meet evenly when assembled. However, making miter cuts on a table saw has the potential to be even less precise than making square crosscuts. Pivoting the miter head actually decreases the amount of support the head provides to the workpiece. As you slide the wood forward and into the blade, it tends to creep along the miter fence. If the workpiece moves at all, accuracy is lost.

To improve your mitering accuracy, add an auxiliary fence to the miter gauge and apply a sandpaper face. The grit will give it better "grip" on workpieces. Make the fence long enough to support the workpiece right up to the blade and provide enough room to clamp a stop block in place on the opposite end. Set up the miter cut so the longer portion of the wood is what you're holding against the miter fence, regardless of whether it is actually the workpiece you want to make or the surplus stock that will be left over afterward.

Another way to better your odds is to orient the miter gauge and workpiece so the end you're cutting will lead the workpiece into the blade rather than trail behind it. This way you can clamp a stop block to the other end of the miter fence to support the back end of the workpiece and keep it from shifting. This arrangement is called a "closed" miter cut. An "open" miter cut occurs when

A quick way to set the miter gauge to cut an angle you've marked on a workpiece is to use the line to set the gauge, as shown. Lock the gauge at this angle, and make the cut with this marked workpiece face down.

Set up miter cuts so the workpiece leads the miter gauge into the blade. This way, you can clamp a stop block to the opposite end of the miter gauge's auxiliary fence to keep the workpiece from shifting when it's cut.

the end you're cutting follows behind the rest of the workpiece and the stop block is clamped to the leading end of the fence instead of the trailing end. In this setup, the blade will tend to pull the workpiece along the fence and away from the stop block during the cut, ruining accuracy. Whether you're cutting an open or closed miter, it's a good idea to clamp the workpiece against the miter fence. This way, you can use both hands for pushing the miter gauge without also having to hold the workpiece steady.

When you need to cut several mitered workpieces to the same length, use a stop block just as you would for making repetitive square crosscuts. Be sure the stop block is sized wide enough so it can support the tip of a workpiece with an end already cut into a miter. Or cut the end of the stop block at an angle to capture the mitered end of the workpiece.

If you have a crosscut sled or sliding miter table, you can use these accessories instead of the miter gauge for cutting miters. With either device, workpieces won't creep during the cut because they are held off the saw table and stationary in the jig. Crosscut sleds usually won't come with an adjustable fence for mitering, but you can make angled cuts by clamping a piece of angled scrap inside the sled to hold your workpiece in the proper position.

Whichever method and saw accessories you use for cutting miters, slow down your feed rate when pushing wood through the blade. You may even want to

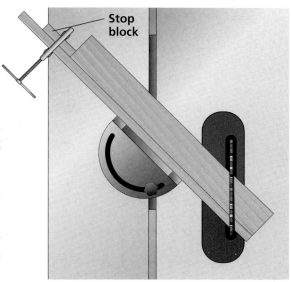

Stop block

Setting up an "open" miter cut, with the miter gauge leading the workpiece, doesn't give you the advantage of using a stop block. As this illustration shows, a stop block won't prevent the workpiece from creeping along the fence toward the blade, ruining your accuracy. If you have no choice but to make an open miter cut, clamp the workpiece to the miter gauge fence for added holding power.

By clamping a piece of angled sheet scrap inside a crosscut sled, you can make a highly accurate mitering device. Add a fence to the angled edge of the scrap for more bearing surface.

Use a bevel gauge set to the angle you want to cut for adjusting the blade tilt. The tilt scale on your saw won't be as accurate a guide (top).

By swiveling the miter gauge as well as tilting the blade, a table saw will cut accurate compound miter cuts (above).

cut just outside your actual layout line to remove most of the waste, then make a second pass along the layout line to cut a smooth, clean edge.

Crosscutting bevels. Beveled crosscuts involve tilting the blade to an angle other than 90° with the miter gauge locked for a square cut. They're easier than miters to perform accurately since the miter gauge isn't pivoted to an angle. The most important issue to keep in mind for bevel cutting is which miter slot to use for the miter gauge. Choose the miter slot that's opposite the direction of the blade tilt. If your saw tilts right, use the left slot, and vice-versa for newer left-tilt saws. This way, the offcut will rest on the saw table as soon as it's cut free rather then end up on top of the tilted blade where it can catch on the blade teeth and kick back.

When cranking the blade to a bevel angle, use a drafting square or a bevel gauge to find the precise degree of tilt. Your saw's bevel scale isn't a precision measuring device. On contractor's saws, the arbor assembly may even twist slightly when it's tilted, regardless of what the bevel pointer reads as the tilt angle. Verify the bevel setting by making a test cut on scrap, then perform the final cut on your workpiece just as you would a square crosscut.

In addition to miter and bevel cuts, you can also make compound miter cuts on a table saw by pivoting the miter gauge and tilting the saw blade. These cuts are common for installing crown moldings. A table saw will cut them accurately, provided you set the bevel and miter angles carefully. Test your setup on scrap and adjust accordingly before cutting your workpiece.

When cutting bevels, arrange the workpiece so the waste will end up below the blade and on the saw table, not above it. Otherwise, the blade teeth are more likely to catch the loose waste piece and throw it off the saw.

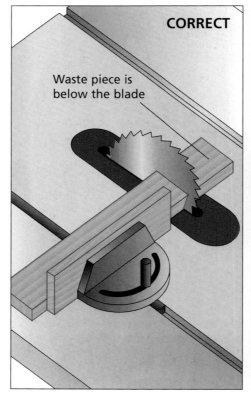

CORRECT

Waste piece is below the blade

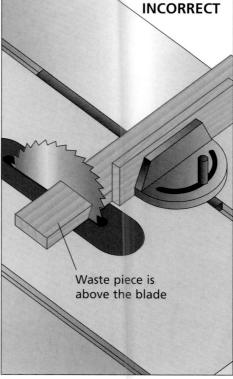

INCORRECT

Waste piece is above the blade

Precision mitering devices

If your table saw suffers from a poor quality miter gauge, take heart. There are a number of precision miter gauges and mitering attachments available through woodworking suppliers that fit most table saws. High-performance miter gauges have large, heavy head stock with longer fences. The protractor scales are larger, making it easier to set the head to a precise angle. Generally, these gauges are designed with preset detents at common miter angles such as 0°, 22.5°, 30°, and 45°, so you won't need to verify the angle setting with a square or a better protractor. Just swivel the head and lock it at the detent. You'll usually have the option to add an auxiliary miter fence accessory to the gauge. These come equipped with a measuring tape and an adjustable flipper stop for making repetitive crosscuts. Expect to pay around $100 for these miter gauges.

A thrifty way to improve the accuracy of a miter gauge is to attach an inexpensive hold-down clamp to the miter head. The clamp presses workpieces down against the miter bar so you can keep both hands off the workpiece and safely clear of the blade. Some activate by squeezing a trigger grip, while others have a handle that tightens down like a screw.

If your woodworking involves a good deal of precision mitering and crosscut work, consider installing a sliding crosscut table on your table saw. These accessories replace the left extension wing and slide on a ball-bearing rail system. They have long, adjustable miter fences that can be set to precise angles. A sliding table not only provides an ample and superior miter fence but also enlarges the saw table so you can crosscut wider or longer workpieces safely and easily. Sliding crosscut tables are available for use on both contractor's and cabinet saws.

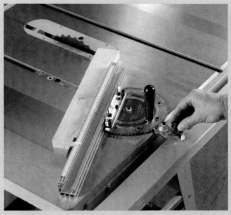

Precision miter gauges offer pinpoint accuracy for mitering. This one has machined detents all around the head.

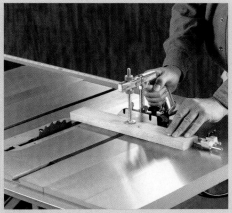

A hold-down clamp anchors workpieces securely against the miter bar and keeps your hands clear of danger.

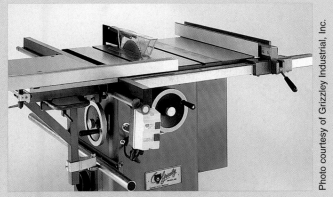

Photo courtesy of Grizzley Industrial, Inc.

A sliding miter table offers the highest level of mitering accuracy along with a stable way to slide large workpieces through the blade.

Chapter 6
CUTTING JOINERY

A table saw's versatility doesn't stop once your project parts are sized to width and length. In addition to performing essential ripping and crosscutting functions, table saws also make wonderful joint-cutting tools, particularly when outfitted with a dado blade. This chapter provides you with a good survey of joints that can be made entirely or in part with a table saw. Be aware that there are scores of different wood joints, and this collection isn't exhaustive. Some joints, such as dovetails, can be made more effectively with a router than a table saw. Other joinery, such as certain traditional Japanese styles, is too complex to be practical here or simply can't be cut with a table saw. However, the joint options we'll cover in these pages should serve most of your general woodworking needs.

Through centuries of woodworking, craftspeople have refined furniture and cabinetry joints to accomplish a few basic purposes. First and foremost, joints serve a structural purpose: they help to bear the loads and resist the natural forces of tension, compression, racking, and sheer that affect two workpieces functioning together. They allow wood to expand and contract with changes in humidity so it doesn't crack or distort. And joinery can contribute a delightfully artistic touch by making the most of contrasting grain, color differentiation, and geometric shape.

To fulfill these purposes, there are numerous ways to join wood. The simplest method is to simply glue two flat parts together and allow the glue bond to do all connective work. Other joints, such as rabbets and dadoes, have interlocking parts so the strength of the wood helps contribute to the connection. These interlocking styles are usually reinforced with glue and screws or nails. Some joints fit together with a third wood member, such as a biscuit, spline, or

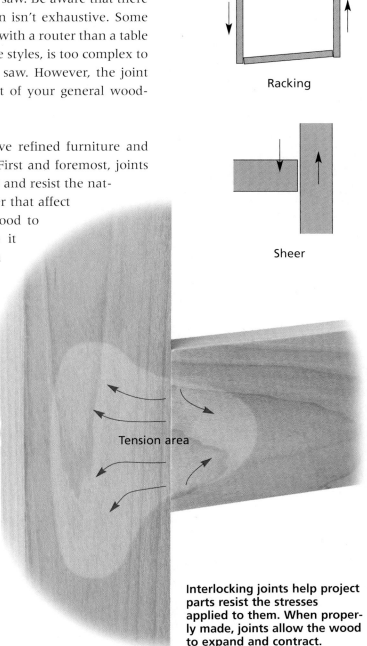

Racking

Sheer

Tension area

Interlocking joints help project parts resist the stresses applied to them. When properly made, joints allow the wood to expand and contract.

WAYS TO CONNECT WOOD JOINTS

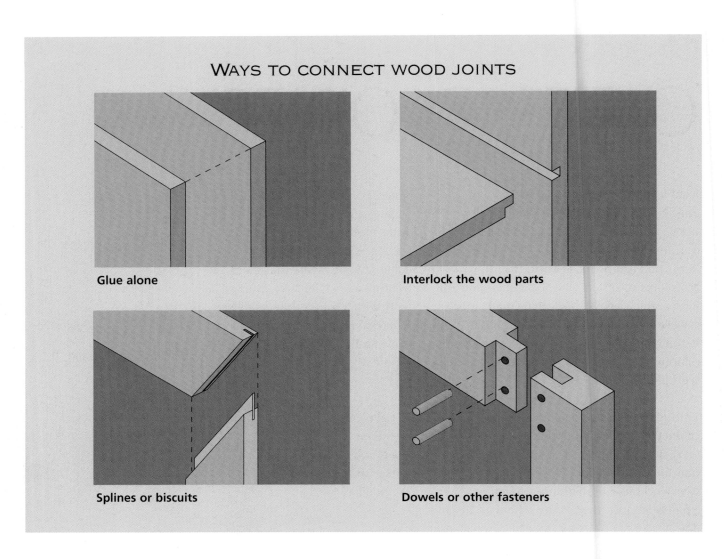

Glue alone

Interlock the wood parts

Splines or biscuits

Dowels or other fasteners

dowel. A few interlocking joints have pins or pegs that lock the parts together in the event the glue bond fails. We'll build examples of all these types in the pages to follow.

Regardless of which joint style you make, the mating parts of a joint must be cut accurately to form durable, snug-fitting connections. If you haven't tuned up your saw in a long while, be sure to do it before you begin cutting wood joints. It is important that the table surface and extension wings form a flat plane, the rip fence is aligned parallel with the blade, and your standard saw blade or dado blade is clean and sharp. Joint cutting is also the time to be meticulous in your fence and blade setups. The tolerance between properly fitting joint parts is extremely small, and often a joint that fits loosely can't be tightened up with shims or strengthened by squeezing on more glue.

You may also want to cut a few blank throat plates for use with your dado blade to form zero-clearance dado inserts. Don't buy the metal throat plates sold for dadoing operations. The blade slot is much too wide for joinery work. Spend the money on a sheet of ½-inch medium-density fiberboard or cabinet-grade plywood instead and make a zero-clearance throat plate for every common dado width.

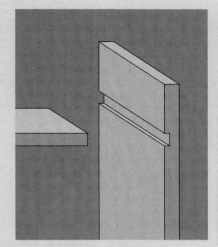

Dadoes run across the wood grain and are commonly used to house another joint part.

Grooves follow the wood grain. They serve the same function as dadoes.

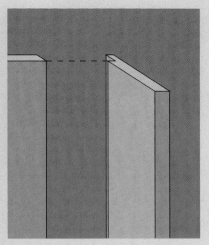

Rabbets may run lengthwise, with the grain, or across the grain. Regardless of the application, they follow an edge or end.

The majority of table saw joints are made with dadoes, grooves, and rabbets, or combinations of the three. These cuts differ from the ripping, crosscutting, mitering, and beveling we've seen so far in that they do not cut a workpiece in two. Dadoes, grooves, and rabbets all are non-through cuts. Technically, dadoes and grooves only differ in terms of how they follow the wood grain. Both cuts form a three-sided channel, but dadoes are cross-grain cuts while grooves run along the grain. You'll often hear the term dado mistakenly used for both long and cross-grain channel cuts. Rabbets form a two-sided cut along the edge or end of a workpiece without regard to grain direction.

Safety

Since non-through cuts don't pass all the way through the workpiece, you'll have to remove the saw's splitter to cut them. The trouble here is that most mass-produced saws have an integrated splitter and guard. Once the splitter is off, the guard goes with it, which leaves the blade completely exposed. The risk of kickback increases dramatically without a splitter in place, and so do your chances of getting cut. One big advantage to investing in an aftermarket blade guard is most work independently of the splitter. Even with the splitter removed, the guard still protects your hands and shields you from dust and chips thrown off by the blade. If your budget won't allow for a better blade guard, do whatever you can to protect yourself from blade exposure. Even a thick scrap clamped to the rip fence over the blade offers more protection than nothing.

Working with a dado blade poses other safety issues as well. Dado blades remove more material than standard blades, so you'll have to apply greater feed pressure to push workpieces through the cut. Instead of forcing the work,

Tune up your table saw before using it to cut wood joints. A saw that is even slightly out of tune will cut joints that don't fit properly.

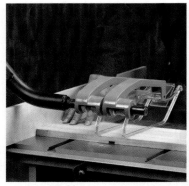

Aftermarket blade guards like this one can be used for making non-through cuts since there's no splitter to get in the way. The guard won't prevent kickback, but it will protect your hands from exposure to the dado blade.

If you don't have a blade guard that works independently of the splitter, you'll have to remove it for making non-through cuts. One way to protect yourself in these instances is to clamp a thick hold-down to the rip fence above the blade to shield it.

which is both harder on your saw motor and more dangerous for you, make the cut in several shallow passes, raising the dado blade higher with each pass. You'll want to use featherboards, clamps, and other hold-down devices to keep workpieces firmly against the saw table and miter gauge or rip fence. Otherwise the increased feed resistance during dadoing operations will tend to lift the workpiece off the saw table as it's cut, making kickback more likely and affecting accuracy.

Cutting dadoes, grooves, and rabbets also means the blade is often hidden from view. Never lose track of the blade's position, and keep your hands clear of the area where the blade will exit the workpiece. The cheapest insurance against injury is to guide the work with a push stick or push pad instead of your palms.

Setting a dado blade

Dado blades require a different setup procedure than standard blades. Since a dado is designed for cutting channels that vary in both width and depth, both of these dimensions need to be set on the dado blade to make an accurate cut. You'll need to mark exactly where the blade will enter your workpiece every time you change the blade width. Wobble-style dado blades are particularly tricky because the blade doesn't spin in a flat orbit like stacked dado blades do, so you can't simply measure off the two outermost cutters.

Before installing a dado blade, use your standard blade to set the arbor spindle parallel to the saw table. You could use the outer cutter on a stacked dado blade, but a standard blade is generally larger in diameter than the dado blade, lending a more accurate reading. Hold a square against the blade and saw table, and adjust the blade to 90°. Then remove the standard blade.

For stacked dado blades, first install the outer cutting blade that rests against the arbor flange. Make sure the beveled teeth face away from the chipper blades you'll install next. (Most stacked dado blades have outer blades milled with teeth that face the same direction.) Slide on the chipper blades next in a combination that will add up to the cutting width you need when combined with the outer two blades. You may need to add a few shims between the chippers to micro-adjust the final cutting width. Shims are often included with the dado blade, or you can use sheets of paper, plastic, or metal with an arbor hole cut in the center. Arrange the chipper blades so the teeth don't contact one another or the teeth on the outer blades. Distribute the chippers evenly around the arbor to help balance the dado when it spins. Install the other outer blade with the bevels facing away from the chippers, and tighten the assembly using both the arbor washer and nut. If your arbor isn't long enough to allow both the washer and nut to fit, pull off a few chippers to make more room. Never saw without the arbor washer in place—it locks the nut.

Before installing a dado blade, adjust your standard blade for squareness with the saw table. When you replace it with the dado, you'll know the dado blade is also square.

Sometimes a joint cut requires a slightly wider setting than you can arrange with the chippers and outer blades. A few paper or metal shims inserted between the chippers and blades can add that bit of extra cutting width you need.

Setting a wobble-style dado blade involves twisting the center hub to the appropriate width marking on the dial. All fine tuning happens here as well—it won't accept shims like a stacked dado blade.

TIP

Cut a piece of test scrap to determine the height and width settings of the dado blade as well as its position relative to the rip fence. Use it to mark a strip of tape on the saw table for easier workpiece alignment.

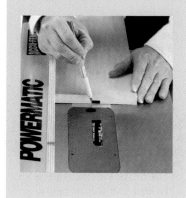

To set a wobble-style dado, follow the manufacturer's instructions for twisting the center hub to set the cutting width. Some blades have a one-piece hub, while others have two-part hubs that twist in opposite directions. The hub has indicator marks for adjusting it to various cutting-width settings. Install the arbor washer and nut, and tighten the dado securely.

For either style dado blade, the next step determines the actual cutting width and depth as well as the location of the cutters relative to the rip fence. If you plan to use a zero-clearance throat plate, follow the same procedure described on page 59 for cutting a blade slot in the throat plate. With the throat plate installed, raise the dado ½ inch above the saw table, and lock the rip fence 2 inches from the blade. Start the saw and cut a groove in a piece of long scrap by sliding the wood along the rip fence. Push the wood a few inches into the blade and shut off the saw, holding the scrap in place until the blade stops spinning. The scrap now becomes an index for blade width, location, and height. Measure the groove width. If it matches what you need, hold the scrap against the rip fence in front of the blade and mark the outer walls of the cut on a piece of tape adhered to the throat plate just in front of the blade. For grooves that are too wide or narrow, adjust the blade width accordingly and make more test cuts on scrap. The tape markings will help you line up the reference marks on your workpieces with the blade. Measure the cutting depth from the scrap, and adjust the blade up or down until more test cuts yield the cutting depth you need.

MAKING A SACRIFICIAL RIP FENCE FOR DADOING

To cut long-grain rabbets with a dado blade, you'll need to bury the blade partially in a sacrificial fence attached to the rip fence. This way, shifting the rip fence exposes more or less blade and serves as an easy way to adjust the width or depth of the rabbet. Working with the dado this close to the metal rip fence requires some careful setup, but it's not an inherently dangerous practice. To make the sacrificial fence, clamp a length of flat, square scrap to your rip fence. Install the dado blade and set it to a slightly wider cut than you'll need. Lower the dado blade below the table, and slide the rip fence over so the sacrificial fence partially covers the dado blade. Lock the fence. Start the saw and slowly raise the cutters up into the sacrificial fence. Be sure the metal fence isn't crossing the cutting path of the blade before you crank the blade up. Stop raising the blade when the blade height matches your intended rabbet depth or width. Never move the rip fence with the saw running, even after you've cut the initial blade recess in the sacrificial fence. Shut the saw down first, then move the fence for adjusting for different rabbet cuts.

Clamp a sacrificial fence to the rip fence and slowly raise the dado blade up into it until the amount of blade exposure matches the rabbet dimensions you want to make.

Make a test cut on scrap, using the miter gauge to feed the scrap past the dado blade. Measure the rabbet, and change the blade height or rip fence settings to adjust the rabbet dimensions.

JOINT-CUTTING WITH A STANDARD BLADE

If you don't own a dado blade, you can still make dadoes, grooves, and rabbets with a standard saw blade. We'll show a dado blade in use for most of the joint-cutting sequences in this chapter because it generally cuts joints more efficiently and cleanly. Really, a stacked-style dado blade set is nothing more than several blades sandwiched together.

To cut a dado or groove with a standard blade, you'll make a series of passes next to one another to remove the waste, mimicking what a dado blade does in one pass. Cut the walls of the dado or groove in the first two passes, shifting either the rip fence (for grooves) or the workpiece's position on the miter gauge (for dadoes) to make the second cut. Remove the waste in between the first two cuts by making successive passes, slicing away a kerf's width of material with each cut.

You can cut rabbets in just two saw passes with a standard blade: One pass with the workpiece standing on edge produces the side wall, or cheek. A second pass with the workpiece flat on its face establishes the rabbet's bottom surface, called a shoulder. The second cut typically slices a waste piece free. When using the rip fence for cutting rabbets, arrange this second cut so the wastepiece falls away on the opposite side of the blade. This way it can't wedge between the blade and fence, and kick back.

Cutting dadoes and grooves

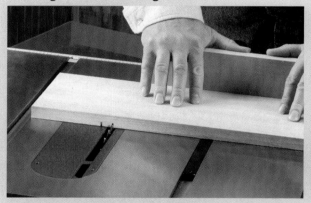

Cut the side walls of the dado first with the blade raised to the proper height. Line up each cut carefully by eye first with the saw turned off. Use the miter gauge to back up cuts.

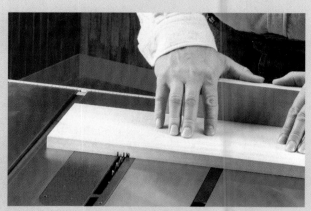

Make a series of passes to remove the waste between the first two cuts to complete the dado.

Cutting rabbets

For rabbets that follow an edge, cut the rabbet cheek with the workpiece standing on edge against the rip fence.

Complete the rabbet with the workpiece face down on the saw table to make the shoulder cut. Be sure to adjust the blade height first, if necessary.

Butt joints. No other joint is faster or easier to make on a table saw than the lowly butt joint. Essentially, all it takes to make a butt joint is a pair of flat, smooth workpiece surfaces. Any pairing of workpiece faces, edges, and ends makes a butt joint. Edge-to-edge butt joints form wider panels from narrower boards. Face-to-face butt joints build thick blanks for table and chair legs or lathe turnings. A butt joint combining the end of one workpiece and the edge of another creates right-angle joints for cabinet face frames. Pair the end of a workpiece with the face of another to make simple shelving or the corner joints for box construction.

What butt joints offer in simplicity they sacrifice in strength. Edge-to-edge and face-to-face joints are stronger than the other options because long face and edge grain responds well to glue. Glue bonds less effectively to the open pores of end grain regardless of the grain direction on the mating surface, and end-grain to end-grain joints are the weakest of all. Whenever end grain is combined with edge or face grain, the glue joint will eventually fail because each workpiece will expand and contract at different rates with changes in humidity.

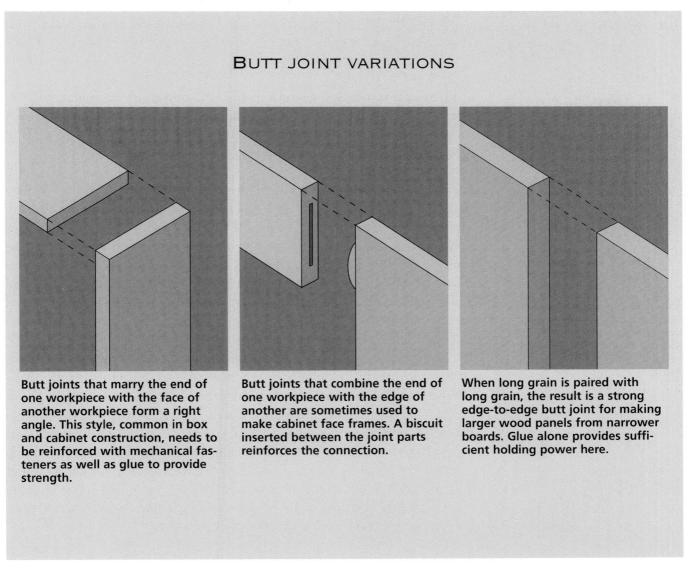

BUTT JOINT VARIATIONS

Butt joints that marry the end of one workpiece with the face of another workpiece form a right angle. This style, common in box and cabinet construction, needs to be reinforced with mechanical fasteners as well as glue to provide strength.

Butt joints that combine the end of one workpiece with the edge of another are sometimes used to make cabinet face frames. A biscuit inserted between the joint parts reinforces the connection.

When long grain is paired with long grain, the result is a strong edge-to-edge butt joint for making larger wood panels from narrower boards. Glue alone provides sufficient holding power here.

Unless a butt joint is connecting faces with faces or edges with edges, reinforce the butt joints with mechanical fasteners such as screws or nails as well as glue.

For edge- and face-glued butt joints, glue alone forms a sufficient bond to keep the joint together. You may want to install biscuits, dowels, or splines to make edge-glued butt joints easier to keep aligned during clamping. Otherwise, wet glue can act as a lubricant under clamping pressure and cause the parts to slip out of position. All other butt joint variations should be glued and reinforced with mechanical fasteners such as screws, nails, staples, dowels, biscuits, or splines driven through both members of the joint.

Cutting butt joints on the table saw is a simple matter of making flat, square rip, and crosscuts using a combination blade or specialized blades for ripping and crosscutting. Check your fence and blade settings carefully for square before cutting the parts. If your blades cut cleanly, you may be able to build the joint as soon as the wood is cut without further tooling. However, it's a good idea to shave off any blade marks and square up the sawn edges using a sharp hand plane or a jointer, especially for edge-to-edge joints bonded only with glue. Flat, square edges here will produce virtually invisible seams.

Wood splines can be used instead of biscuits to join edges with ends. Despite their slender thickness, splines add considerable strength to the joint.

Splined butt joints. Splines are a good way to convert the flat mating surfaces of a butt joint into interlocking parts. Splines also contribute additional wood surfaces inside the joint for more glue surface. As you'll see in other joints to follow, more gluing surface area adds strength.

Splines are thin strips of wood or plywood inserted into a pair of matching slots that cross the butt joint. One slot is cut into each member of the joint, usually with a standard blade in a table saw. The width of the spline is typically equal to the thickness of the workpieces. Spline thickness should be about one-third the board thickness. So for butt joints in ¾-inch stock, splines should be milled ¾-inch wide and ⅛- to ¼-inch thick. Larger splines don't add much to joint strength, and they can even weaken the joint if the spline slots are too wide or deep.

To make splined butt joints, cut the spline slots first. Center the slot locations on the thickness of the joint parts when possible for greatest strength. Using either a standard saw blade or a narrow dado blade, set the cutting height to one-half the spline width plus ½₂ inch more to provide a "well" for excess glue. This height will center the spline across the joint. Cut edge and end spline slots with workpieces standing on edge or on end against the rip fence. For end cuts on narrow workpieces, clamp a runner to the workpiece so it rides on top of the rip fence to provide additional support, or use a tenoning jig (see opposite page). Saw slots into the faces of workpieces using either the rip fence or miter gauge as you would to make standard rip or crosscuts.

Use a tenoning jig to cut spline slots in the ends of narrow workpieces. Center the workpiece carefully over the blade, or the joint won't align when assembled.

To cut spline slots along the edge of a workpiece, use the rip fence. Set the blade height slightly higher than necessary to provide a well for excess glue to seep into.

Cut the thin splines from solid stock, ripping them in strips off the edge of the workpiece. Adjust the rip fence carefully so the spline is the correct thickness to fit the slots.

TIP

When cutting end- or edge-grain spline slots, it's important that the slot is exactly centered on the workpiece. You can ensure centered slots by passing the workpiece along the rip fence twice—one pass with each face against the fence. This way, any misalignment of the cutter will still make a centered, although slightly wider, spline slot.

Cut the spline stock after you've cut the slots so you can carefully match the spline proportions to the slots. If you're making splines from solid wood, rip them off the edge of a board. A pushing jig can make this operation safe and easy when you have to rip multiple, narrow splines (see page 75). Choose a piece of spline stock with a thickness that matches the spline width you need. If you accidentally cut splines that are too wide or thick to fit the slots, do not try to rip or joint them to correct the error. The spline proportions will be too small to make these kinds of machining corrections safely. Reset the rip fence for a narrower cut, and rip new splines instead.

Rabbet joints. Rabbets are two-sided channels cut along the edge or end of a workpiece. Their shape forms an offset tongue that can be used to form partially interlocking joints. Inside this rabbet channel, the cut that forms the side of the tongue is called the **cheek**, and the other cut forms the rabbet's **shoulder**. When the ends or edges of two workpieces are milled with matching rabbets and combined at right angles, the result is a double rabbet joint. You can also cut a rabbet with a cheek wide enough to completely conceal the flat end or edge of another workpiece and make an overlap rabbet joint. Both overlap and double rabbet joint styles are often used for building boxes and cabinet carcases. Overlap rabbets are especially useful because the rabbets hide the end grain of back and top panels. Secure these joints with a combination of glue and brads, nails, or staples.

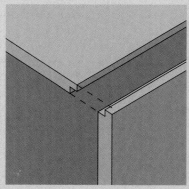

Cheek

Shoulder

A third rabbet joint style—the shiplap—mates pairs of matching rabbets to form an interlocking flat joint for panel construction. You'll see shiplaps used on back panels where the boards aren't glued together. The stepped effect of the joint hides board edges when they shrink. Shiplaps are a stronger option than edge-glued butt joints for building panels because the cheeks and shoulders are self-aligning if they're cut carefully, and they contribute more surface area for glue.

Rabbets can be cut on a table saw using either a standard blade or a dado. Dado blades require a bit more setup time, but one

RABBET JOINT VARIATIONS

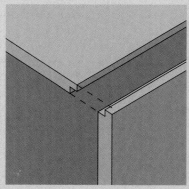

Double rabbet joints combine a pair of matching rabbets to form a right angle. These joints are commonly used in casework construction.

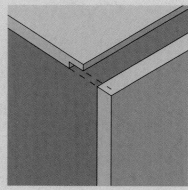

Overlap rabbet joints consist of one rabbeted workpiece with a tongue that fits over the thickness of the mating workpiece.

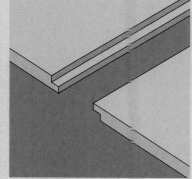

Shiplap rabbets marry a pair of matching rabbets to form a larger flat panel. The interlocking rabbets add more surface area for glue than a butt joint.

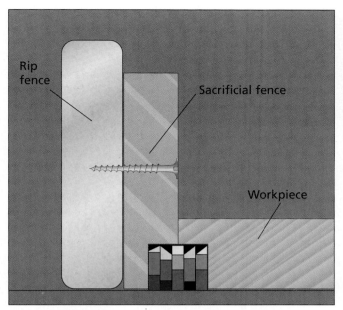

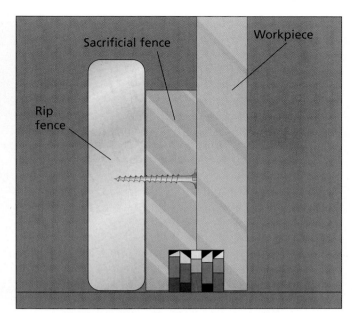

To cut rabbets along the edges of a workpiece with a dado blade, set the blade partially in a sacrificial fence and pass the board face down over the blade. If the rabbet follows a wide end or edge, feed it by hand against the rip fence.

When rabbets follow a long edge of a narrow workpiece, you can run the workpiece on edge against the sacrificial fence. For wide workpieces, make the sacrificial fence taller than shown here to provide sufficient support.

CUTTING END RABBETS WITH A STANDARD BLADE

To cut a rabbet into the short end of a workpiece with a standard blade, make the cheek cut with the workpiece clamped on end in a tenoning jig.

Switch to the miter gauge for making the shoulder cut. Use a zero-clearance throat plate in the saw to keep the small waste piece from dropping down into the blade slot when it is cut loose.

A dado blade can also be used to cut short end rabbets. Back up the workpiece with the miter gauge, and bury the blade partially in a sacrificial rip fence. Since this is a non-through cut, both the rip fence and miter gauge can be used in tandem safely.

pass over the cutter forms both the cheek and shoulder cuts without resetting the blade height or rip fence position. To cut rabbets with a dado blade, install a sacrificial fence on the rip fence and set the blade width ⅛ to ¼ inch wider than the rabbet cheek will need to be. Raise the blade and move the rip fence until the amount of blade that projects out from the fence equals the shoulder and cheek dimensions. For rabbets that follow the edge of a workpiece, pass the workpiece through the dado blade on its face like a rip cut. Install a featherboard directly over the dado blade and a second featherboard to the saw table adjacent to the blade to keep the workpiece tight against the table and fence as you make the cut. You can also cut edge rabbets with workpieces standing on edge, but orient the workpiece so the tongue is cut outside the dado—not between the fence and blade. Test your setup on scrap before cutting your actual workpieces to be sure the rabbet proportions are accurate.

Use the miter gauge to support workpieces for cutting rabbets on board ends. Make the cut with workpieces face down. Clamp a stop block to the rip fence and use the rip fence as a way of indexing the cut, just like you would for making repetitive crosscuts (see page 92).

Cutting rabbets with a standard saw blade is a two-step operation. One cut forms the cheek and a second cut makes the shoulder. Mark the rabbet shape on the workpiece before you cut it to serve as an index for setting the blade height and fence position. It doesn't matter which cut you make first, but if you're milling a series of rabbets on a number of workpieces work efficiently by making all like-sized cuts before resetting the saw for the second cuts.

For edge rabbets, form the cheek by standing the workpiece on edge against the rip fence. Then reset the fence and cut the shoulder with the board flat on the saw table. Arrange this second cut so the wastepiece will fall on the side of the blade opposite the fence. Do not make the shoulder cut with the waste piece between the blade and rip fence, or it could wedge inside this tunnel when it's cut free and kick back. Be careful to reset the blade height as well if you are cutting overlap rabbets where the cheeks and shoulders are different sizes.

If you're cutting rabbets on short board ends, you'll need to cut the cheeks with the workpiece standing on end. When the workpiece is long or particularly narrow, clamp the board in a tenoning jig and make the cut this way rather than running it on end against the rip fence. If it rocks or teeters, the workpiece could bind the blade and kick back. You can also make this short end cut safely by attaching a tall auxiliary rip fence and supporting the workpiece from behind with a wide piece of scrap. Cut the shoulder with the workpiece on its face and against the miter gauge. Use a stop block clamped to the rip fence to index the shoulder cut (see page 122), or line up the cut by eye. Either way, do not use the rip fence to support the workpiece during the shoulder cut.

Rabbet-and-dado joints. When rabbets are paired with dadoes, the combination creates a strong, interlocking joint with several woodworking applications. Rabbet-and-dado joints are often used to lock the ends of bookcase shelves into the cabinet sides. The shelf ends receive the rabbets and the bookcase sides are dadoed across their faces. Typically the rabbet tongues are one-half the thickness of the workpiece they're milled into.

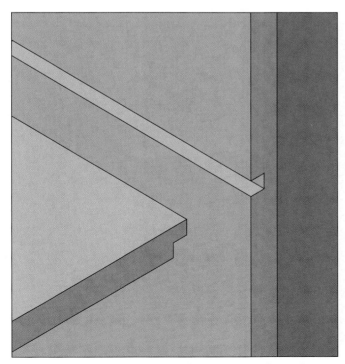

Rabbet-and-dado joints combine the interlocking characteristics of a tongue in a slot with the increased glue surface area contributed by the rabbet.

Bare-faced tongue-and-dado joints are similar to a conventional rabbet-and-dado joint with a much thinner rabbet tongue.

A variation on this joint, commonly called a bare-faced tongue and dado, features a thinner rabbet tongue that's just one-quarter the thickness of its workpiece. The rabbet fits into a ¼-inch-deep dado. This joint makes a strong connection on drawer box corners when the tongue side of the rabbet faces into the drawer cavity. The drawer front and back pieces are rabbeted while the drawer sides receive the dadoes. In this orientation, the interlocking nature of the joint keeps the joint from pulling apart when drawers are opened and closed. By cutting the rabbet tongues thinner than a conventional rabbet dado joint, more of the short-grain material is left on the drawer sides near the ends to strengthen the connection. Be aware that the end grain of the drawer sides will show from the front, so choose these drawer joints when you're building drawers with an additional drawer face that covers the end grain.

Cut the rabbets for a standard rabbet dado joint using the same procedure as discussed on page 110 for cutting rabbets. A regular saw blade or a dado blade are both suitable for cutting these rabbets, but a dado blade makes quicker work of cutting the ¼-inch-deep dadoes in one pass. For standard ¾-inch stock, make the dadoes ⅜ inch wide to house the rabbet tongues.

It doesn't matter which half of the joint you cut first, the rabbets or the dadoes. If you're just beginning to cut joinery, you may find it helpful to cut the dadoes first, then make the rabbet tongues slightly thicker than necessary and pare them down with a chisel or rabbeting plane until they fit snugly but go together without forcing the parts. Trim the ends of the tongues a hair shorter than ¼ inch so there's a bit of extra room in the bottom of the dado for excess glue to migrate. As your skills increase, you'll be able to cut rabbets accurately to size just using the table saw. Regardless of your skill level, it's always a good idea to make test cuts on scrap first to inspect your saw settings.

Make the narrow dado for a bare-faced tongue and dado using a standard saw blade. Support the workpiece with the miter gauge to make the cut.

Cut the tongue slightly shorter or the dado a bit deeper than needed to leave a small open cavity inside the joint. Excess glue will pool here while allowing the joint to close completely.

Use a standard saw blade with a ⅛-inch kerf to cut the dadoes in a bare-faced tongue and dado. On ¾-inch stock, this is as wide as you'll need to make the dado for a sturdy connection. Cut the slots a bit deeper than necessary to capture excess glue in the bottom of the joint. Then cut the rabbets by making a pair of cheek and shoulder cuts with a standard blade, or cut the whole rabbet to shape with a dado blade in a single pass along the rip fence.

Tongue-and-groove joints. Tongue-and-groove joints feature a rabbet tongue centered along the edge or end of one workpiece that fits into a matching dado on the face, edge, or end of the other joint part. The interlocking nature of this joint makes it a good structural choice for joining cabinet face frame or door frame stiles and rails. You could install shelving inside a bookcase with tongue-and-groove joints, and the shoulders on either side of the tongue will hide the dadoes. Tongue-and-groove joints form strong, self-aligning connections when you're assembling panels to make table tops or hiding their end grain with "breadboard" ends. Even if the joint isn't glued, such as you'll find on the "floating" back panels of traditional furniture, the tongues and grooves keep gaps from appearing as the wood expands and contracts.

Lay out the joint parts so the tongues are one-third the thickness of the workpieces. If you're inserting the tongue of one workpiece into the face of another board, such as with bookcase shelving, make the tongue extend just halfway into the thickness of the dadoed part. In cases where the dadoes for the tongues follow the edge or end of a workpiece, make the tongues and dadoes a bit longer and deeper—½ inch for joints in 1× stock.

A dado blade mills these joints quickly and easily. Start with the slot-cutting

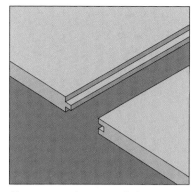

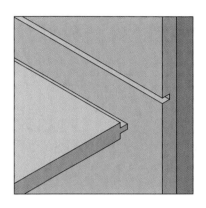

Tongue-and-groove joints usually follow workpiece edges (above), but sometimes they also cross a workpiece face (below).

Make the groove for a tongue-and-groove joint with a dado blade. If the groove follows an edge, as shown here, it's easy to center the slot automatically on the workpiece thickness. Simply make it in two passes against the rip fence, flipping the workpiece from one face to the other.

Cut the tongue for a tongue-and-groove joint using a sacrificial rip fence and dado blade. Set up the blade so a pass along each face of the workpiece cuts both sides of the tongue.

work (either dadoes or grooves, depending on the grain direction). For ¾-inch workpieces, set your dado blade for a ¼-inch cutting width and raise it to the appropriate height. Mill the slots against the rip fence when they follow the edge. Use a tenoning jig for cutting end slots, or cut these against the rip fence with a tall auxiliary fence installed and backing up the cut with a wider piece of scrap to steady the workpiece. Cut cross-grain dado slots with the miter gauge guiding the workpiece.

Once the slots are cut, cut the tongues. The dado height you set for cutting the slots is nearly perfect for cutting the tongues to length, but lower it ⅟₃₂ inch so the tongues won't bottom out in the slots. Install a sacrificial fence on the rip fence and slide the fence over until it just "kisses" the blade. In this position, the dado should cut a cheek and shoulder accurately in one pass with the blade fully exposed. Cut one side of the tongue on a piece of test scrap, then flip the scrap to the other face and make a second pass to complete the tongue. Check the fit of the tongue in a groove. The parts should slip together easily with just a slight bit of resistance. A fit that's too snug could break the tongue or the slot walls and even starve the joint of glue when the final parts are assembled.

Often your test fit will require a bit of refinement. If the tongue is too thin, reposition the rip fence a hair closer to the dado blade and cut another tongue on more scrap. NOTE: In this situation, you may have to lower the blade completely and cut a blade recess into the sacrificial fence to cut a narrower shoulder (see page 105). Use the previous test scrap as a quick reference for resetting the blade height. Correct overly thick tongues by moving the fence slightly further away from the blade to cut a wider shoulder. A single tap on the fence might shift it just enough to perfect the fit.

Housed dado joints. A fast way to form interlocking joints for shelving is to leave the shelf ends flat and square and simply fit them into dadoes that match the shelf thickness. This way, the shelves are "housed" in the uprights. Even though the joint parts form a strong connection that will bear a lot of weight, it's still a good idea to glue and nail the connections. Otherwise the joint could pull apart if the shelves bow under load. Glue and nails also add some rigidity to the bookcase carcass. One downside to this joint is that the dado will show along the front edge. You can hide the joint behind a face frame, solid-wood edging, or veneer edge tape.

To build these joints, set up the width of the dado blade carefully. The dadoes should be a hair wider than the shelf thickness so the parts fit together easily but not so wide that a gap will show. Here's a situation where a few paper or metal shims slipped between the chipper blades on the dado could provide just the bit of extra "wiggle room" needed for a good fit. Set the blade height for about one-third the thickness of the workpieces receiving the dadoes. Experiment on test scrap to test the fit of the shelves in the dadoes before cutting dadoes across the actual workpieces.

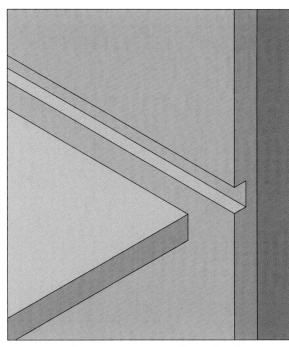

Housed dado joints connect a flat-edged or ended workpiece with a matching dado.

Blind dado joints. For bookcases without face frames, blind dadoes are a convenient way to hide the joints along the front edges. The dadoes of these joints are cut to match the thickness of the shelving, just like a housed dado, only this time the dadoes stop short of the front edge of the dadoed workpieces. The front corners of each shelf are notched so the shelf can wrap around the stopped dadoes and still line up with the front edge bookcase carcass.

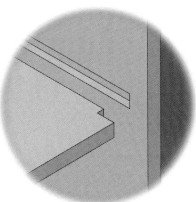

Blind dado joints (above) feature a stopped dado instead of one that passes all the way across the workpiece. When assembled, the joint looks like a butt joint with the dado concealed inside.

Paper or metal shims (left) inserted between the chippers of a dado blade can help refine the fit of a housed dado joint. This is especially helpful when building plywood joints, because the material is often manufactured slightly undersized in thickness.

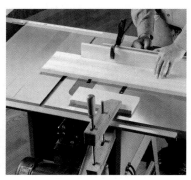

To set a blind dado cut, clamp a stop block behind the blade so the distance from the front of the blade to the block equals the dado length.

Feed the workpiece over the blade until it touches the stop block. Use the miter gauge to back up the cut.

Cutting stopped dadoes on the table saw is an easy maneuver, but it requires careful setup. Set the dado width using shims, if necessary, to be sure the shelving will fit snugly but without binding in the standards. Raise the blade to cut dadoes one-third of the way through the carcase standards.

Blind dado joints won't permit you to gang-cut two standards at once like housed dado joints (see Tip, page 119), but you can still measure and mark the dado locations on one wide workpiece, then split it into two standards before cutting the dadoes. Or lay the standards next to one another and mark the dadoes across both workpieces so they'll match.

Make the stopped dado cuts with a stop block clamped behind the dado blade on the saw table. As you push each standard through the dado with a miter gauge, it will only pass partway over the cutters before stopping at the block—thus the "blind" aspect of the cut. Set up the stop block by holding the standard against a long auxiliary miter fence. Slide the two forward until the leading edge of the standard just touches the front dado teeth. Determine the dado length by measuring across the width of the standard and subtracting the amount of material you'll want to leave along the front edge (¾ inch is typical). Without moving the workpiece, plot this distance across the dado blade, starting from where the standard and dado teeth meet, and measuring back. Clamp a wide stop block to the saw table so its front edge meets your measurement. Remove the standard and make a test cut on scrap the same width as the standards to test your setup.

If the dado stops where it should, mill the standards. Be sure to mark the dado width on the saw table so you can align each cut accurately (see page 104). As

Square up the front rounded end of the dado with a chisel to form the blind end.

Trim off the front corner of the mating piece that will fit into the blind dado. Size the notch so the workpiece will be flush with the front edge of the dadoed workpiece.

you complete each pass over the dado, shut off the saw and wait until the blade stops spinning before pulling back the miter gauge and standard to set up the next cut. Once all the dadoes are cut, square up the curved portion of each dado with a sharp chisel.

Short, narrow bookcase shelving might allow you to cut the front corner notches with workpieces standing on edge against the miter gauge. Mill the notches in one pass with the dado blade partially buried in a sacrificial fence. If the shelves are large and unwieldy, cut the notches with a hand saw or jig saw instead.

Lap joints. Lap joints combine a wide rabbet with a dado or a wide pair of dadoes together so the workpieces cross at full width and the faces of the mating parts are flush. Typically, lap joint dadoes are cut halfway through the thickness of their parts. They're also cut wide enough to house a rabbet tongue or a matching dado that's as wide as the mating workpiece. Lap joints may connect workpieces of equal or differing thickness, depending on the application, but the former type are more common. When the workpiece thicknesses aren't the same, of course only one pair of workpiece faces will be flush. Choose lap joints for building strong table and bench frameworks where legs meet stringers and aprons. The joints are interlocking and provide large surface areas for gluing.

Lap joints take many forms, as shown on page 120. Corner half-laps combine two matching rabbets arranged at 90°. T half-laps couple an end rabbet on one

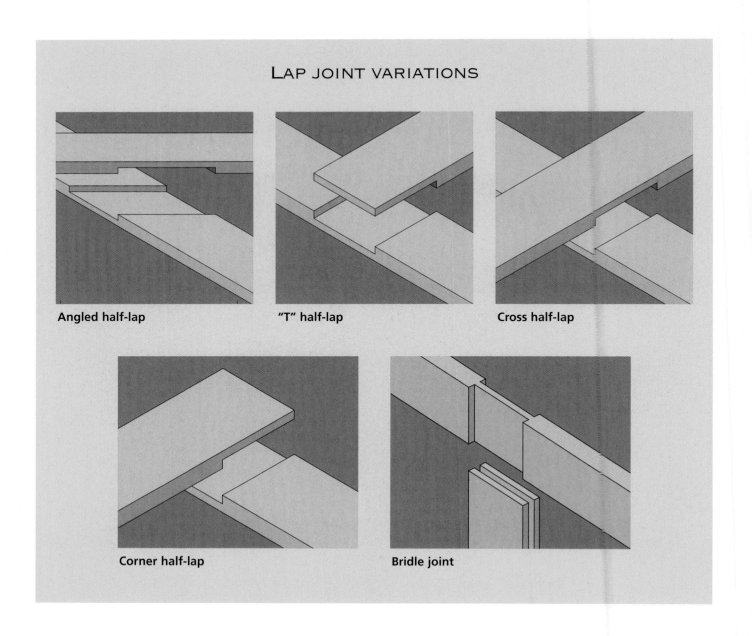

LAP JOINT VARIATIONS

Angled half-lap

"T" half-lap

Cross half-lap

Corner half-lap

Bridle joint

workpiece with a dado on the other workpiece. Cross half-laps and angled half-laps form an intersection where two wide dadoes lock together at 90° or another angle. Another less common lap joint hybrid is the bridle joint. Here, a pair of wide dadoes are milled into opposite faces of one workpiece. A deep end slot is cut into the mating workpiece to create two outboard tongues. The tongues fit around the dadoes.

There are no special cutting techniques for making lap joints. Set the dado blade for a wide cut to remove waste material more quickly, and mill the dadoes or trim the rabbet cheeks and shoulders in several side-by-side passes. For lap joints on workpieces with matching thicknesses, you can use the same blade height setting to machine both workpieces if you set the cutting height carefully. To help minimize tearout and to provide more workpiece support, back up the dado cuts with an auxiliary miter fence. Be sure to mark the dado cutting width on the saw table so you can line up the cuts accurately (see page 104).

A dado blade and miter gauge make quick work of cutting the notched half of a bridle joint. Make the notch in a series of side-by-side passes.

Cut the tongue of the lap joint as you would a wide rabbet using a tenoning jig and miter gauge. Make the tongue in two passes with a standard blade—one for the cheek and another for the shoulder. Or, use a dado blade and nibble the waste away.

Lap joints unavoidably form cross-grain connections. If the workpieces expand and contract significantly, the glue bonds will eventually fail. Reinforce the glue joint with dowels, screws, or bolts driven though both members if the joints will be subjected to moisture or extreme twisting or racking stresses.

Mortise-and-tenon joints. Mortise-and-tenon joints are arguably the strongest examples of interlocking joinery. Furniture builders have used them for centuries in situations where strength and stress resistance are paramount. You'll find mortise and tenons used most commonly to attach chair and table legs to aprons, rails, and stretchers. These critical connections are subject to the full gamut of racking, sheer, and tension forces as furniture is moved about and loaded down. Mortise and tenons keep chairs and tables standing tall by taking full advantage of those factors that contribute most to joint strength—namely large surface areas for glue and fully interlocking parts.

The tenon portion of a mortise-and-tenon joint can be cut with a standard blade or a dado blade.

Typically, only the tenon portion of these joints can be made on the table saw. Tenons are the centered, long-grain tongues on the end of one workpiece that fit into a matching slot—called a mortise—in the other workpiece.

Tenons have two to four pairs of cheeks and shoulders, depending on the joint style, and all these cheek and shoulder faces form gluing surfaces. As far as proportions go, tenons are usually one-third the thickness of the workpiece. Their length is determined mostly by the width of the workpieces that house them and the joint style itself—mortise and tenons take many forms. Some tenons stop halfway or less through the mortised workpiece, while other joint designs extend the tenon all the way through and even beyond the mortised workpiece. "Through" tenons are often wedged in place from the opposite end or across their width for greater strength. Even joints with fully concealed tenons are frequently locked with pegs or dowels driven through the mortise walls and into the tenons. The cross connection ensures that the joint will stay together in the unlikely event that the glue bond fails.

The process for cutting tenons on a table saw is straightforward and simple to do with either a standard saw blade or a dado blade. Cheek and shoulder cuts can be made with a standard saw blade in two ways: First, cut the tenon cheeks and shoulders with the workpiece lying flat on the saw table and against the miter gauge. Use a stop block clamped to the rip fence to index the first shoulder cut, then form the cheek by making side-by-side passes over the blade out to the end of the workpiece. Flip the workpiece over to cut the second shoulder and cheek. If the tenon has cheeks and shoulders on the board ends as well as the faces, stand the workpiece on edge against the miter gauge to cut the narrow cheeks. You may need to change the blade height for cutting the end cheeks, but keep the rip fence stop block where it is so the shoulder cuts line up all around the tenon.

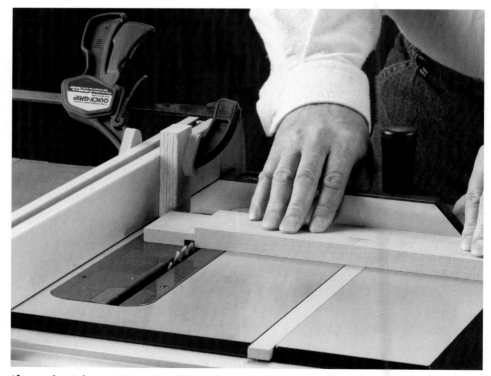

If you don't have a tenoning jig or dado blade, you can cut tenons with a standard blade and miter gauge. Start with the shoulder cuts indexed off a stop block clamped to the rip fence. Remove the waste out to the end of the tenon in side-by-side passes.

A quicker method for cutting long cheeks is to stand the workpiece on end against a tenoning jig. Set the blade height so the teeth cut to the shoulder line, and be sure to account for the thickness of the blade when lining things up so it cuts on the waste side of the tenon layout line. If the tenon has four shoulders and cheeks, cut the narrow end cheeks with the workpiece face clamped against a tall auxiliary fence on the miter gauge.

Once you've made all the cheek cuts, trim the shoulders using the miter gauge with the workpiece laying flat or on edge. Install a stop block on the rip fence to index these shoulder cuts. Be sure to reset the blade height carefully so you trim just to the saw kerfs you cut for the cheeks.

A dado blade cuts tenon cheeks and shoulders more efficiently than a standard blade because it removes more material with each pass. Use the same multiple-pass technique as you would with a single blade to cut tenons with the workpiece flat on the saw table. Clamp a stop block to the rip fence to index the shoulder cuts, and make these cuts first. Then remove the remaining waste in a series of additional passes working out to the end to form the cheeks. Stand the workpiece on edge to cut end cheeks, if necessary.

One style of mortise-and-tenon joint, often called a bridle joint (see diagram, page 120), can be cut entirely on the table saw. The mortise is an open slot on one end rather than inset, so it can be cut on the table saw with the workpiece standing on end against the rip fence. Other mortise-and-tenon joints feature mortises set in from the workpiece ends. These must be hollowed out with

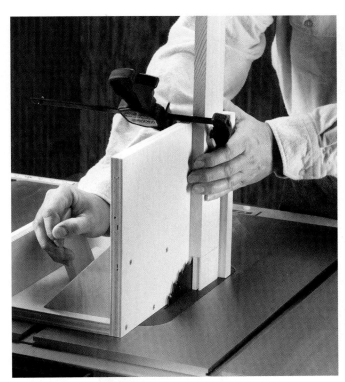

A second method for cutting tenons with a standard blade is to make the long cheek cuts with the workpiece clamped on end in a tenoning jig. Set the blade height so it cuts each cheek in one pass.

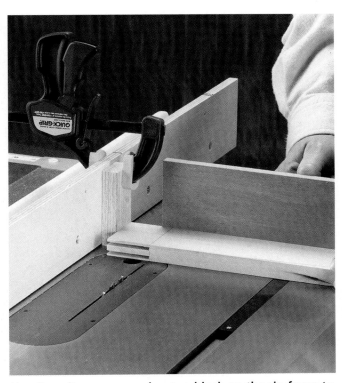

Use the miter gauge and a stop block on the rip fence to trim off the waste in a pair of shallow shoulder cuts. Position the stop block so the workpiece clears it before making contact with the blade.

chisels or by cutting the slots with a drill press, router, or dedicated mortising machine with hollow chisel bits.

Finger joints. When you're building a chest, drawers, or boxes, finger joints can make the corner connections both strong and attractive. This joint combines equally spaced "fingers" with matching slots, so it has the look of through

A dado blade cuts tenons more efficiently than a standard blade. Start with the shoulder cuts and make a series of passes out to the tenon end.

If the tenon has short shoulders on the ends as well as the faces, cut these with the workpiece on edge against the miter gauge.

Make mortises on a drill press by drilling a series of holes in the mortise area with the workpiece backed up against the drill press fence. Use a Forstner bit to bore these holes.

Clean up the walls and square the ends of the mortise with sharp chisels. Make the mortise opening slightly oversized so the tenon fits into it with just a bit of friction, but not extra play.

dovetails without all the angles. It gets its strength principally from the gluing surfaces sandwiched between the fingers and slots. Finger joints are remarkably easy to make with a dado blade and a shop-made jig. If you build the jig carefully, the joint should slide together smoothly with no further tooling.

Build this joint starting with the jig. It consists of an auxiliary miter fence with a pin attached that matches the size of the joint slots. The pin is offset one "finger width" away from the dado blade and acts like a spacer for creating the finger and slot pattern. Clamp a fresh auxiliary fence to your miter gauge, and install a dado blade. Set the width of cut to match the finger pin width. You can choose any width you like, but ¼-, ⅜-, and ½-inch fingers are typical. Raise the blade so it will cut the full depth of the pins—they should be as tall as the mating workpiece is thick. Use an auxiliary miter fence that's about 18 inches long and at least 6 inches wide. You'll be cutting the joint workpieces on end, so the fence must be tall enough to provide adequate support.

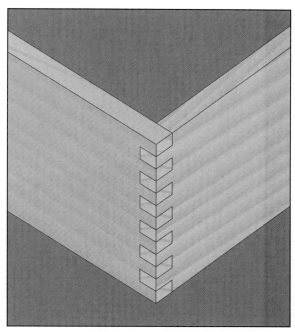

Finger joints combine a series of matching pins and slots to create an attractive and sturdy connection.

With the fence clamped in place so it's roughly centered on the miter gauge, cut one slot through the fence. Glue a hardwood pin into this slot so it projects ¾ inch in front of the fence. Reset the fence on the miter gauge, sliding the pin exactly one finger width away from the dado blade. The spacing here is crucial. If you have a piece of extra hardwood pin stock, use this as a spacer between the pin on the jig and the dado blade to set the fence position. Screw the fence to the jig again, and try the following procedure on

Make the finger joint jig by clamping a new auxiliary fence to your miter gauge and cutting a finger slot through it with a dado blade.

Install a hardwood pin into the slot and shift the fence over so the distance between the pin and the dado blade matches the pin thickness. Measure this distance carefully, and fasten the jig to the miter gauge.

Make the first pin on the workpiece by setting its edge against the jig pin and passing it through the blade. Hold or clamp the workpiece to the jig, whichever affords you better control.

Once the first pin and slot are made, slip the slot over the jig pin and cut the second pin and slot. Repeat this process to cut the rest of the pins and slots across the workpiece.

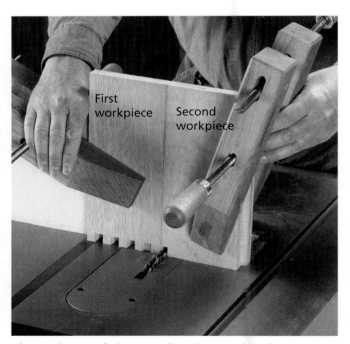

First workpiece   Second workpiece

The mating workpiece needs to have a slot along its edge so it will mesh with the first workpiece. To set up this cutting pattern, fit the first pin of the first workpiece between the blade and jig pin to fill this space, and butt the second workpiece against the first. Now the blade will cut a slot on the second workpiece instead of a pin. Make this cut, remove the first workpiece, and cut the remaining pins and slots in the second workpiece.

scrap before you cut your actual workpieces. If the joint parts don't fit properly when you finish cutting your scrap test pieces, the culprit is an inaccurate gap between the blade and jig pin. Reset the fence slightly to perfect the gap spacing, and try the test cuts again.

To cut the fingers and slots, butt the first workpiece against the pin with the board standing on end. Clamp or hold it firmly to the fence, and slide the jig through the blade to cut the first pin. If the workpiece is clamped firmly, slide the jig back across the blade to prepare for the next pass. If you're holding the workpiece instead, remove it and slide the jig back. Reposition the workpiece on the jig so the slot you've just cut straddles the jig pin, then cut the second pin and slot. Repeat this procedure to cut all the remaining pins and slots on this workpiece end. When you're finished, flip the board end over end to cut a matching pattern of pins and slots on the other end.

Form the mating part of the joint by fitting the first slot you cut in the first workpiece over the jig pin so one pin on that board fills the gap between the blade and the jig. Butt the other workpiece against its mate. This way, the second board will receive a slot along the edge for the first cut and not a pin. Slide both workpieces over the blade to cut the initial slot, then remove the first workpiece. Slip the slot of the second workpiece over the jig pin, and make a second pass to cut its first pin. Repeat the slot-cutting technique across the board, then flip it end over end and use the first workpiece again to set the first slot cut.

When all the joints are cut, they should fit together snugly, but without force or gaps between the slots and pins. If so, the joints are ready for glue.

Splined bevel and miter joints. End-grain to end-grain surfaces often come together when you join workpieces with either miters or bevels. Glue alone can't form a strong connection because the open wood pores wick too much glue away from the mating surfaces. If you're making mitered picture frames or boxes with beveled corners, a spline inserted between the joint parts strengthens the connection immensely. Splines can also add a bit of decoration to the joint if you make them from wood that contrasts with the joint parts.

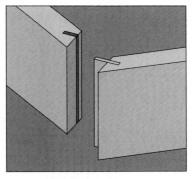

Splined bevel joint

Both beveled and splined miter joints can be cut easily on the table saw. If you're building with ¼-inch-thick stock, the splines only need to be ⅛-inch thick, so you can cut spline slots with a standard blade. For thicker workpieces, switch to a dado blade to cut wider slots. In both of these joint styles, the splines extend the full length of the joints, but the kerfs are cut in different fashions. For splined bevels, the workpiece rests face down and is cut with the blade tilted. The workpieces of a splined miter joint stand on their mitered ends against a simple jig that supports them at an angle for the slot cuts.

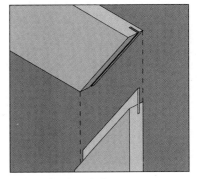

Splined miter joint

For splined bevel joints that form 90° corners, first cut the beveled ends on the workpieces with the blade tilted at 45° (see page 96). To cut the spline slot, set the workpiece on the saw table with the beveled angle facing down. Tilt the blade to 45° so it faces the beveled workpiece. Raise the blade so it projects

Use the rip fence to index the location of the spline slot on the beveled end of the workpiece. Cut the slot with a standard blade using the miter gauge to support the workpiece from behind.

⅜ inch above the table. Slide the rip fence to the side of the blade opposite its tilt direction. Using the rip fence as an index for the end of the workpiece, adjust the fence and workpiece so the blade will cut into the beveled end of the workpiece at its inside corner. Back up the workpieces with the miter gauge and an auxiliary fence when you cut the spline slot in each part.

Making the spline slots on a miter joint requires cutting the workpieces along their mitered ends against the rip fence. There's no way to tackle this cut safely by simply feeding the workpiece along the rip fence and over the blade. Instead, clamp the workpiece flat against a larger backer board so the mitered end is aligned with the bottom edge of the backer. A piece of plywood makes good backer material. Attach a strip of wood to the backer board so it braces the mitered workpiece at 45°. With the blade set square and raised to ⅜ inch, run this jig against the rip fence equipped with a tall auxiliary fence to cut the spline slot. Adjust the rip fence before you make the cut so the blade is centered on the thickness of the workpiece, which centers the spline on the joint.

Rip splines from the edge of a piece of ¼-inch lumber, just as you would for building splined butt joints (see page 108). Cut the splines carefully, and sand the faces if necessary so the splines slide smoothly into the joint slots. Glue and clamp the joints, then trim the splines flush with a hand saw.

Locate the spline in a beveled spline joint so it's near the inside corner. This position keeps the outside corner from breaking when the joint is stressed.

To cut spline slots for a mitered spline joint, fashion a tall jig with a clamp and fence to hold the workpiece at the miter angle securely. Slide the jig along a tall auxiliary rip fence to cut the slot.

Glue splines into their slots, leaving the splines a bit long. When the glue dries, trim the splines with a fine-toothed back saw and sand them flush.

Chapter 7
OTHER TABLE SAW TECHNIQUES

You can safely use your table saw for other woodworking tasks such as cutting large sheet materials, shaping moldings and coves for trim work, and disk sanding.

Cutting sheet goods

Manufactured sheet goods such as plywood, particleboard, and medium-density fiberboard (MDF) are excellent materials for making large furniture panels. They have no definite grain pattern, so they're more dimensionally stable than solid wood, and you won't have to glue up individual pieces to obtain the panel size you want. The downside to sheet goods is that most full-sized sheets are heavy to lift and unwieldy to wrangle around the shop and up onto the saw. You can cut them accurately and safely on a table saw, provided you consider the following guidelines.

First, provide plenty of sturdy workpiece support. For full-sized sheets, you'll want to set up a pair of roller stands behind the saw to catch workpieces as they leave the machine. Anchor these stands with sand bags or cinder blocks to keep them from shifting

To rip sheet goods safely, set up one or two roller stands behind the saw to catch the material as it leaves the saw.

during cutting. For crosscutting long panels, set up side support. A long work table is an excellent choice in these situations. It should provide support all along the side of the saw as well as beyond into the outfeed area.

Be sure to use a guard and splitter when cutting sheet materials. You'll typically have to stand away from the saw to start these cuts, and the size and weight of the material make it more difficult to control the cut. If the workpiece veers away from the fence during ripping operations, kickback is likely. Safeguard yourself as best you can with a guard and splitter.

Often, you'll work with sheet materials that form square or rectangular shapes rather than long, thin strips. It may be more difficult to decide whether your next cut is a rip cut or a crosscut when sizing down a square. Here's a good rule to follow: Whenever possible, saw with the longer edge against the rip fence. This orientation becomes more important to follow with longer workpieces or shorter ends. If the length is more than twice the width, use the miter gauge and auxiliary fence or a crosscut sled to make these crosscuts instead of running the shorter edge against the rip fence.

Finally, if the sheet material is too heavy to lift, cut it into more manageable portions with a circular saw or jig saw instead. Size the parts a little wider or longer than necessary, then make your finish cuts at the table saw on the smaller workpieces.

A work table provides a sturdy means of outfeed support, provided the table top is slightly lower than the saw table.

For crosscutting long sheet goods, set up a work table or other stable support device alongside the saw to keep the panel from tipping off the machine.

Ripping full-sized sheets. The procedure for ripping sheet stock is similar to ripping board lumber, but you'll begin the cut further back and more to the left of the saw. The objective is to feed sheet stock into the blade with your right hand, while keeping the workpiece held tight to the fence with your left hand.

For full-length rip cuts, extend your rip fence by adding a long, stout auxiliary fence. Make the fence at least 1 to 2 feet longer than the rip fence, so it extends far enough off the back of the saw to provide plenty of side support when most of the sheet has passed through the blade. It's also a good idea to lock the rip fence down to the saw table on the outfeed end with a clamp if your fence design only clamps to the front fence rail. An extra clamp on back keeps the fence body from deflecting during the cut.

If a panel is too large to handle easily, it's too big to be cut safely on a table saw. Cut it down to more manageable size with a circular saw instead. Cut the work pieces slightly oversized, then trim the smaller panels to final dimensions on the table saw.

To begin the cut, tip the leading edge of the sheet up and onto the infeed side of the table. Position yourself behind the sheet near the left corner with your left hand wrapped around the long outside edge and your right hand gripping the end of the sheet. Feed the sheet into the saw, pushing forward with your right hand, in a straight line with

A good way to keep sheet goods held securely to the saw table is to clamp a large hold-down to the rip fence. Adjust the hold-down so the panel slides easily across the saw but without extra play.

Start a rip cut on large sheet materials by standing behind the rear corner of the sheet and pushing with your right hand. Keep the material pressed firmly against the rip fence with your left hand.

the blade. Apply diagonal force toward the rip fence with your left hand. Keep your eyes on the joint between the rip fence and the workpiece as soon as the workpiece enters the blade. It doesn't take much shifting on your part to skew the sheet away from the rip fence, so make any changes in hand or body position gradually. Keep the sheet sliding flat on the saw table at all times.

Increase your feed rate once the cut has begun, keeping your motions fluid and the sheet moving forward. As the back end of the sheet nears the front of the saw, shift yourself from the left corner of the sheet around to the back edge, moving your right arm so it guides the workpiece portion between the blade and the rip fence. Move your left hand closer to the left corner of the sheet so you can maintain some diagonal pressure between the sheet and the rip fence. When the distance between the rip fence and the blade is wider than 1 foot, it's safe to use your right hand to feed the workpiece past the blade for the entire cut. Use a pushstick in your right hand for narrower workpieces.

Once the workpiece is cut in two, continue to guide the workpiece past the blade with your right hand or with a push stick. Use your left hand to hold the wastepiece against the table so it doesn't drift into the blade. Both the wastepiece and the workpiece should be supported as they leave the saw table by way of roller stands, an outfeed table, or a helper.

Cutting coves with a standard blade

Cove molding with smaller profiles is readily available at any home center, but

As the cut progresses, move your body behind the sheet. Eventually your right hand should push the material between the fence and blade through the cut. Use a side support device for cutting panels larger than this one.

you won't find moldings with radii larger than about ¾ inch. For larger profiles, you can use your table saw as a makeshift shaper and mill your own cove molding. It's easy to do with a simple parallelogram jig and a fine-toothed plywood blade. The technique involves passing the wood over the blade at an angle and shaving the cove profile in lots of shallow passes, raising the blade ¹⁄₁₆ inch with each pass. By varying the angle of approach on the blade, you can change the shape of the cove. Profiles ranging from steep and tight curves to gentle and wide arches are possible, depending on the angle you choose.

Setting up a cove cut requires the use of an adjustable parallelogram jig. Build one from straight strips of 2-inch-wide scrap. Make the long sides 4 feet and the short ends 1 foot. Attach the parts with short carriage bolts, washers, and wing nuts so you can adjust the jig shape by hand. The jig will establish the angle you'll need to cut a cove with a specific curvature and width.

TIP

Oftentimes, sheet material is covered with thin wood veneer or melamine. These surface materials are prone to chip or tear out on the bottom face during a cut. An easy preventive measure is to saw with a zero-clearance throat plate installed, and saw with the "good" face up. You may want to switch to a triple-chip blade designed for cutting melamine, or use a blade with more than 80 teeth for crosscutting veneered plywood.

Cutting coves. Install a fine-toothed plywood-cutting blade. An inexpensive blade with hardened steel teeth produces smoother cuts than a general-purpose carbide blade with fewer teeth, but both blade types will work. Draw a curved layout line on the end of the workpiece you'll use to make a piece of molding, and raise the blade so the tips of the teeth line up with the highest part of the curved line.

A pair of straightedges clamped at an angle to the blade are all it takes to turn your saw into a tool for shaping moldings.

Open the parallelogram jig so its inside edges match the width of the cove lay-out line. Set the jig on the saw table and over the blade, then twist the jig left or right until the inside edges touch the front and rear blade teeth at the same time. Work carefully to find this position—the jig angle establishes your angle of approach for cutting the profile.

Set a bevel gauge against the front edge of the saw table and lock it to the same angle formed by the parallelogram jig. Do not shift the jig out of position when you do this. Once the gauge is set, remove the parallelogram jig. Replace it with a flat-edged piece of scrap long enough to stretch across the saw table at the jig angle. It will serve as a fence for guiding the cove cuts. With the bevel gauge

Mark your workpiece to the cove shape you want to cut, and raise the blade to match the deepest part of the cut.

Open the parallelogram jig so the inner opening match-es the width of the cove profile. Pivot the jig on the saw table so its inside opening touches the front and back blade teeth.

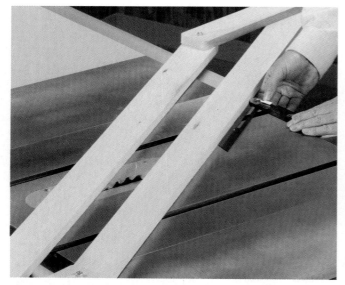

Without shifting the jig's position, use a bevel gauge to record the jig angle on the saw. Lock the gauge and remove the jig.

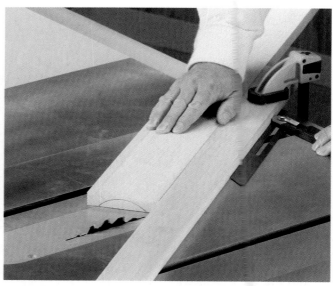

Clamp a straightedge to the saw table at the jig angle. Position the inside edge of the straightedge so the cove lines up with the blade. Set the workpiece in place, and clamp a second straightedge behind it, parallel with the first straightedge.

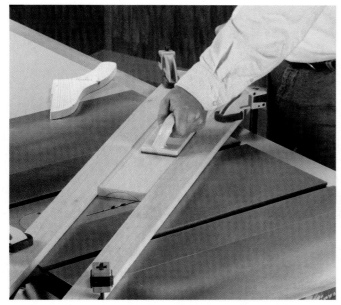

Cut the cove to shape in a series of shallow passes, starting with the blade teeth about ⅟₁₆ inch above the saw table. Increase the cutting height no more than ⅟₁₆ inch with each pass.

You can also cut partial coves by shifting the straightedges so the blade cuts partway into one straightedge. Cut the partial cove the same way as a full cove in many passes of increasing depth.

still braced against the front of the saw table, set the cove workpiece against the inside edge of the angled fence. Slide the gauge, fence and workpiece together and left or right until the front blade teeth intersect with one end of the cove layout line. Clamp the fence securely to the saw table.

Clamp a second fence parallel to the first, using the cove workpiece as a spacer between the fences. You could use just one fence, but the tunnel formed between the two will keep the cove workpiece aligned all along the cut. Check the tunnel spacing on both sides of the blade with the workpiece to be sure it will slide easily, but without extra play all along the cut.

Cut the cove shape, starting with the blade lowered until just the tips of the teeth project above the table. Make each pass slowly, using a pair of push sticks to keep your hands safely above the workpiece. Raise the blade ⅟₁₆ inch with each pass until the blade shaves away the entire layout line.

You can also cut partial coves using this procedure by burying a portion of the blade in the fence. Once you've established the fence angle using the parallelogram jig, adjust the bevel gauge to this angle. Hold the fence against the bevel gauge and clamp the fence down. Raise the blade into the fence until the width of the blade that's exposed matches the width of your partial cove layout line.

Milling trim with a molding head

Molding heads consist of a heavy center hub that accepts sets of interchangeable molding cutters called knives. Knives come in many different profiles so you can make both conventional and more unusual types of trim molding. In the long run, a molding head can save you money over buying premilled mold-

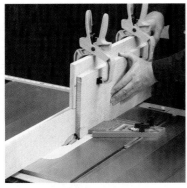

For edge profiling with a molding head, stand the workpiece against a tall auxiliary fence attached to the rip fence. Clamp a second board to your workpiece to ride along the top edge of the auxiliary fence. This "runner" board keeps the workpiece from diving down into the molding head.

ings, and you'll have the unique advantage of making moldings from any wood species you like.

This said, exercise extreme caution when using a molding head. Molding heads, like dado blades, don't make through cuts. You won't be able to use your stock guard and splitter with these devices, so kickback is a greater concern. They also have just two to four knives that are responsible for all the cutting action, and these knives can be easily overwhelmed if you remove too much material in one pass. Overloading a molding head leads to kickback. It's also crucial to tighten the knives securely on the hub before you make a cut. Even if you're using the same knife setup from a previous operation, check the retaining screws that hold the knives in place to be sure they're still snug.

Limit your exposure to the knives as much as possible. Instead of using a metal dado blade throat plate with an overly wide blade opening, raise the molding head into a zero-clearance throat plate made of wood (see page 59). This way, only the knife profile will protrude above the saw table. Install a sacrificial wood fence to the rip fence for setting the cutters flush to the fence, and raise the blade into the wood fence slowly to create a recess for the knives just as you would a dado blade for cutting rabbets (see page 111). Clamp a featherboard to the saw table next to the knives to press workpieces firmly against the rip fence during each cut.

Always keep the molding head oriented so the workpiece is milled on the side of the knives opposite the rip fence. Cutting a profile with the workpiece sandwiched between the molding head and rip fence increases the risk of it jamming in this tunnel area and kicking back on you. As a rule of thumb, if the cutters are spinning partially inside of a sacrificial rip fence, you've got a safe setup.

Sanding on a table saw

It's easy to convert a table saw into a stationary sander by simply installing a sanding disk. The disk is a flat steel plate for mounting adhesive-backed sandpaper disks. It installs on the saw arbor like a saw blade and fits through the throat plate opening. Some styles have a tapered face as well as a flat face for sanding chamfers, or you can tilt the arbor slightly to perform this function. To sand safely, hold workpieces firmly against the saw table and remove stock on the infeed end of the sanding disk where it spins back into the saw table. This way, the abrasives and direction of spin help hold workpieces down. Sanding on the outfeed end could allow the disk to catch and throw the workpiece upward.

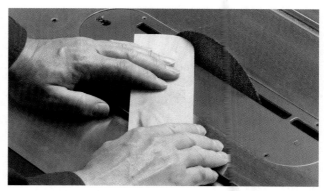

Hold workpieces flat on the saw table and sand on the inked end of the disk.

SHAPING NARROW WORKPIECES WITH A MOLDING HEAD

If you're making narrow moldings, shape the profile along the edge of wider stock, then rip the molding free with a standard blade. This keeps your hands a safer distance from the knives and makes it easier to control the cuts. For those instances where you must shape the edge of narrow workpieces, make a shroud around the knives to hold workpieces as you feed them through the blade. Here's how: Attach a sacrificial rip fence, then fasten another scrap with a flat edge to the wood fence to form a top hold-down. Position the top support on the wood fence so its height off the saw table matches the width of the work-

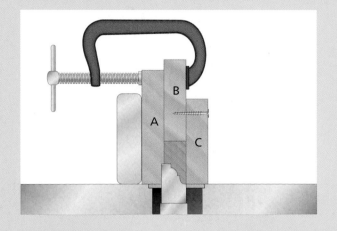

pieces you'll be milling. The top support thickness should match the workpiece thickness. Fasten a side support to the top support to act like a solid-surface featherboard alongside the cut. Make the top and side supports shorter than the length of the workpieces so the workpiece ends will protrude out from the shroud on both ends. This helps you maintain a better degree of control over the workpieces while feeding them into the knives.

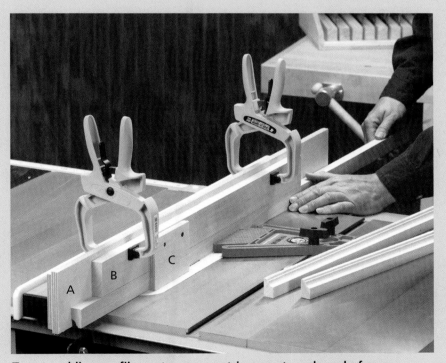

To mill profiles with this blade shroud, set the knives to make shallow passes of ⅛ inch at a time. Feed workpieces into the shroud with a scrap of workpiece stock that fits into the shroud opening. Push the workpiece all the way through before shutting off the saw and removing the pushing scrap. If you're milling lots of strips with this setup, feed them end to end so the next workpiece serves as a push stick for the previous one.

To cut molding profiles onto narrow strips, create a shroud of scrap pieces attached to the rip fence like this. The scrap closest to the rip fence (A) keeps the molding knives away from the metal rip fence. A second scrap over the knives (B) acts as a hold-down, and its thickness should match the workpiece thickness. A third scrap in front (C) keeps workpieces from drifting away from the rip fence during shaping. Feed strips one after the next so they act as push sticks.

CONTRIBUTORS

Delta Machinery
www.deltamachinery.com
800-223-7278

DeWALT
www.dewalt.com
800-433-9258

Felder USA
www.felderusa.com
800-572-0061 (West Coast)
866-792-5288 (East Coast)

Grizzly Industrial, Inc.
www.grizzly.com
800-523-4777

HTC Products Inc.
800-624-2027

Laguna Tools
www.lagunatools.com
800-234-1976

ReTool
www.re-tool.com
952-898-7160
A special thanks to Allen Grimm at ReTool
for his contribution of photo props and
location.

Shopsmith, Inc.
www.shopsmith.com
800-543-7586

INDEX

Also from

CREATIVE PUBLISHING INTERNATIONAL

ISBN 1-58923-093-0

ISBN 0-86573-577-8

ISBN 1-58923-139-2

CREATIVE PUBLISHING INTERNATIONAL

18705 LAKE DRIVE EAST
CHANHASSEN, MN 55317

WWW.CREATIVEPUB.COM